The Politics of Washing

College

The Politics of Washing

Real Life in Venice

Polly Coles

ROBERT HALE · LONDON

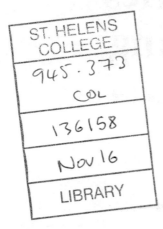
© Polly Coles
First published in Great Britain 2013

ISBN 978-0-7198-0878-4

Robert Hale Limited
Clerkenwell House
Clerkenwell Green
London EC1R 0HT

www.halebooks.com

A catalogue record for this book is available from the British Library

10 9 8 7 6 5

Printed in Great Britain by Ashford Colour Press Ltd

'Guardarobieri in crisi!
Zaini dei turisti troppo pesanti!
Mal di schiena al Palazzo Ducale.'

('Cloakroom attendants in crisis!
Tourists' backpacks too heavy!
Back pain at the Ducal Palace.')

(Headline from *Il Gazzettino* of Venice,
June 2008)

'J'avoue que dans l'Amérique j'ai vu plus que l'Amérique.'

('I admit that I saw in America more than America.')

(Alexis de Tocqueville)

'[Are we] reading into Greek poetry not what they have
but what we lack?'

(Virginia Woolf)

To F who wished Venice would 'just sink'
and ended up a Venetian himself.

To A and O who knitted and gossiped up and
down the Grand Canal.

To G who was so brave.

To Andrea, whose patient and selfless commuting back
and forth across Europe meant all of this could happen.

Contents

Acknowledgements

MY AFFECTIONATE THANKS to the following friends who read this book at different points in its evolution and offered their encouragement and invaluable criticism:

George Misiewicz, Jenny Condie, Patrick Marnham, Liz Jensen, Geraldine Bedell and John Francis Phillimore.

Amongst the many Venetians, born and adopted, who have, in one way or another, been a part of the making of this book, my warm thanks go to Enrico Palandri, Giovanni Levi, Donata Grimani, Pisana Visconti, Giampaolo Rinaldo, Marie Brandolini, Piero Maestri, Riccardo Held (for help with dialect), Jane Caporal (who so generously and enthusiastically taught me how to row Venetian style) and to Holly Snapp, without whom, quite literally, none of this would have happened since she not only introduced me to my agent but also, many years ago, to my partner.

I am very grateful to my agent John Beaton, who has been so cheerfully industrious on my behalf; to Clive Brill, for his help along the way (and a pen) and to Alexander Stilwell and Nikki Edwards, my editors at Robert Hale.

Last of all, my love and gratitude go to my parents, Bruce and Sally Coles, who brought me to Venice in the first place.

A Short Venetian Glossary

Acqua alta: high water
Barene: mudflats, exposed only at low tide
Batela: flat-bottomed boat of the Venetian lagoon
Bricole: wooden posts tied together and sunk in water to mark the navigable channels in the lagoon
Calle (plural: *calli*): Venetian street
Campo (plural: *campi*): square or public space
Cantiere navale: boatyard
Caorline: flat-bottomed lagoon boats
Capanna (plural: *capanne*): beach huts
Carabinieri: national military police of Italy
Forcola: carved wooden structure, slotted into the side of lagoon boats, on which the oars rest whilst rowing
Fondamenta: street running along a canal
Forestieri: forest dwellers, people from terraferma
Gondolieri: the people who row gondolas
Imbarcadero: boat stop (mooring)
La Serenissima: the most Serene Venetian Republic
Marinaio: boatman (or woman) on the vaporetto
Moeche: soft-shelled crabs: a Venetian delicacy
Il nonno: grandfather
Pasticceria: a cake shop
Piano nobile: the main (noble) floor of a palazzo

Poppa: the rear of a boat

Prua : the front (prow) of a boat

Rio: a canal

Rio terà: an earthed in canal

Sandolo: a flat-bottomed boat that is lighter and smaller than a gondola

Sanpierota: a flat-bottomed boat originally used for fishing

Spiaggia libera: the free beach, where anyone can swim or sunbathe, without paying

Riva: bank (of a river or canal)

Terraferma: the mainland (dry land)

Topo: a slightly rounder lagoon boat, originally used for fishing and the transportation of fruit and vegetables

Trenitalia: Italy's national train company

Vaporetto (plural: *vaporetti*): water bus

Voga: rowing

Prologue

THE FIRST YEAR I spent in Venice with my family was a time of vivid novelty for all of us. I could have predicted very little of what happened. Before I actually lived there, my image of the place was like everyone else's: a waterborne city of quite extraordinary beauty and strangeness. But as the months went by and I began to learn the patterns of daily life, what absorbed me was not so much the beauty as the relationship between the city and its inhabitants. I began to notice the ways in which people live there – in the present, but also in intimate relation to history.

The reality of Venice, where millions of lives have amassed over centuries, day by unexceptional day, creating living reefs of memory and experience, runs radically counter to the image of Venice as a museum-fossil. The small surviving community of residents in the city sometimes strikes me as hopelessly disparate: a raggle-taggle of 'indigenous' Venetians, foreigners and Italians (that is all those whose families have not been in the city for generations); but the fact remains that almost everybody here is united by the desire to give this city another chance to live. Against all the odds they continue to believe that Venice still offers a vibrant model for the good life, even for a future.

When I first began to show people the stories that fill this book they said that I was casting my net too wide; that it was neither fish (history or travelogue) nor fowl (a personal account of my year-in-an-exotic-place). But that, for me, is the point: you cannot live in a place that is three parts myth to one part daily life and not engage with it in ways that range from the banally pragmatic: how to get the shopping home through a foot of water? – to the profound: how would all the world be if it were freed from the tyranny of the car? What effect does water have on the soul? How might a child conceive of his place in the present when growing up in an environment so palpably chiselled out of centuries of history?

So this book is a maverick thing. It is the story of the year my family lived in Venice; it is about the city, its corners and backwaters, and it is about the Venetians themselves and the ways in which they navigate their extraordinary home. But, most of all, it is a plea to halt the daily violation of one of the earth's most precious treasures by unregulated tourism; to preserve not only its stones but its living culture; to allow Venezia to become, once again, just a bit more normal.

PART 1: Getting Away

I SPEND MY last night in England in casualty. Earlier today some friends, eager to help in the last frantic push to move our family of six to a new life on the other side of Europe, took my children off to an adventure playground, leaving Alberto and me to the packing. Lily, who is nine, lost her grip on the jungle gym, crashed awkwardly to the ground and broke her ankle. This is a small disaster: we are about to leave for the last remaining city in the world where the only way of getting from one place to another is on foot.

In casualty at the country hospital a disturbed young man is ranging around the waiting area. He is heavily built, with a ragged beard and a long, dark, shabby overcoat. He has more of the Russian novel about him than small town Midlands, and his distress and anger fills the space with an alarming stench that is perhaps the stench of his fear, though it quickly becomes ours too as he bellows for his psychiatrist, pacing the walls like a man imprisoned, then suddenly, shockingly, kicking the thin doors of the prefab building so hard that they shake. Eventually, a nurse comes in and briskly pulls a curtain around Lily and me.

'That's better,' she says.

And as the man continues to crash about on the other side of the flimsy partition, I wonder if out of sight is out of mind when it comes to violent paranoid schizophrenics.

The day after tomorrow we will be in Venice, the city that has fed into generations of foreign dreams. My fantasy of escape, predictably enough, assumes a place without the mad, the sad, the inadequate, the just plain difficult. I have visited Venice often and, like so many millions of others, have wandered around open-mouthed in a state of soft-focus wonder, but I have no notion of what it will really be like to live there. I am setting out armed with little more than a handful of clichés, some fond holiday memories and a great deal of optimism. I also have four children in tow.

The following morning, Alberto and I close the door on our house in the small hamlet where we live and the children climb into the green VW van. Once they are seated, we stuff the last of the luggage in around them. Lily, who sits by the window, her foot in pristine plaster, is incarcerated in her own zimmer frame all the way across France. Her twin brother Roland is buried somewhere beside her under blankets and bicycle helmets and whatever else has suddenly, at the last minute, seemed indispensable to a life on water. The two other boys, twelve-year-old Michael, and Freddie, who is six, are lost under still more domestic miscellany – soft toys, frying pans, sleeping bags – in the back row.

Our friends and neighbours have come out to wave goodbye and for five minutes, as we spin off down the country lane in the sparkling September sunshine, towards a new life, it all feels a bit like the movies.

Late the following afternoon, the green van staggers into Mestre, the last mainland stop before Venice and part of a sprawl of industrial developments and petrol refineries strung out along the edge of the Venetian Lagoon.

We park on the roof level of a multi-storey car park next to the station. As the children uncrumple themselves from the travel mulch in the back of the van, I walk slowly across the scorching tarmac and lean on the parapet. The hot air is sickly sweet with traffic fumes; stretched out below me is a tangle of glittering railway lines and overhead cables, empty rolling stock, parking lots, warehouses, factory yards. I lift my face to the sun and breathe out: the long drive is over.

Then I squint across the mess of rooftops to the bright waters of the Lagoon. On the horizon, very small, I can see the towers and domes of Venice: an ancient, improbable labyrinth of a city stuck out at the end of a 4-kilometre causeway, on the edge of the Adriatic Sea. Now it is time to make the final push and get there but we are, as usual, late, so we decide that Alberto should go ahead to meet the landlord, leaving me, with the children and the luggage, to come on behind.

Here, for the first time, we experience what I later come to recognize as the Venice Effect. This is the cruel illusion that you have arrived at the city when, in fact, there is still a very long way to go. In order to reach Venice you have to complete the Three Tasks.

The First Task is to find somewhere to leave your car. For those with cash, there are various car parks, ranging from the solid, middle-range Tronchetto to the high-budget San Marco, which takes you as close to Venice as any car gets: the bus station at Piazzale Roma. For those who are either too hard up or just cheapskates – and we fall into both these brackets, depending on the month – there are the back streets of Mestre. Parking here may involve running the gauntlet of irritable locals, sick of seeing a car left dormant for weeks at a time outside their house and knowing full well where its apparently invisible owner holes up.

The Second Task is to transfer your many, heavy belongings on to a train or a bus. Once this has been done, there is a temporary illusion of speed and ease as you travel quickly and smoothly across the causeway to the station of Santa Lucia, on the edge of the city. At this point, however, you have the Third Task and the greatest logistical challenge. Here, all wheeled transport other than the trolley disappears and you have the problem of how to get your luggage and, in our case, a large and partially disabled family to your final destination.

Of course there are the *vaporetti*, but *vaporetti* are buses and where would you find a bus driver willing to take you to the front door and then carry the bags up several flights of stairs to your flat?

If the building has a water entrance on a canal, you can hire a boat or commandeer a friend, but these were all things I learned later. Arriving – and surviving – in Venice that September day, I still had no idea of such organizational subtleties.

There is no more total translation from one world into another than the ten-minute train ride across the Lagoon from Mestre to Venice. Already, in the quiet waters you see from the train window, there are subtle clues about the real life, past and present, of the city. To the left of the causeway, there is a small island, overgrown with mangy scrub. This is San Secondo, once a graceful and busy complex of renaissance buildings – a convent and its church; an inn for travellers heading to the city; a boatyard and gardens and vegetable plots: a miniature version of the waterborne city ahead. But now not a single building remains standing on San Secondo; it is just a muddy pimple alongside the railway track and is rapidly dissolving into obscurity.

There are, though, other signs of a continuing life. Fishing nets are hung raggedly about on posts sunk into the muddy floor of the Lagoon. There is still the constant, centuries-old flux of traffic criss-crossing back and forth along the deeper channels: delivery boats, taxis, *vaporetti*. And there are still people rowing the ancient, flat-bottomed lagoon boats – the *sandoli*, the *gondole*, the *caorline* – standing up and pushing forward on long oars, through the shallow waters, as they have for more than a thousand years.

I don't know any of these things on that baking afternoon in early September, when our train comes to a standstill in the station, and anyway I have more pressing practical matters to deal with.

First, I have to heave Lily down from the train and set her on the dusty station platform. She leans heavily on her little zimmer frame, her broken foot lifted limp off the ground, as the other passengers walk briskly away. Heat scintillates over the disappearing tracks and the three boys pass down the bags. Then, each one shoulders a rucksack and as much else as he can manage and we begin our halting progress across the station concourse – luggage and able-bodied persons – 3 metres forward. Stop. Then back to drag more bags and piggy-back Lily over the same 3 metres. Bags and able-bodied forward. Stop, drag and piggy-back. Bags, able-bodied forward. Stop, drag and piggy-back.

We carry on in this way for twenty minutes, by which time we have covered about half the length of the concourse and are red-faced and sweating. This is when a small woman in a shiny blue trouser suit emerges from her office. She has been watching us. She has a metal *Trenitalia* badge pinned to her lapel and a worried look on her sharp little face.

'Signora,' she says, with anguish. 'Where are you going?'

I tell her.

'Signora, how are you going to get there?'

Her tone is not complicit: she does not identify with this bedraggled Englishwoman hauling her children and belongings across a foreign station and does not, therefore, feel empathy, but she does see that it is a situation to be dealt with. She directs us to the left luggage office with instructions to borrow a wheelchair. I feel myself being cravenly, gushingly grateful, but still she does not smile. The welfare of children is not a matter of mere personal sentiment in Italy: it is a question of public duty. This is why if your child leaves the house without a coat, a hat, a scarf or gloves on a winter's day, you will be told off vociferously by a string of indignant strangers. This is why the woman in the station office does not see in me a sister struggling under duress, but a wrong to be righted.

Once Lily is installed in her *Trenitalia* wheelchair, and most of our luggage has been piled on her lap, we roll smoothly out of the station and down a concrete side ramp, acrid with the stench of urine. At the bottom, we turn the corner and find ourselves on a wide pavement, overlooking the Grand Canal.

All of a sudden, I smell the mineral sea, hear the soft cacophony of voices and footsteps, and feel the sharpness of sunlight off water. We have arrived.

Number 3460 Calle del Vin is a fortress-like palazzo, a great, dour, stone building which stands at the corner of a gloomy alley lined with similar tall, dark, ancient buildings. Calle del Vin is a street to be passed along, not lingered in, but the façade of the palazzo gives on to a bright, wide canal, lined with shops and bars – a pleasant, busy thoroughfare that somehow manages to keep out of the tourist mainstream.

Built in 1460, the palazzo spent the first 400 years of its existence in the hands of two wealthy families; the first were Venetian aristocrats, the second, Flemish merchants. Once, the palazzo had been famed for its large and beautiful gardens; now, it is divided into five apartments, with a number of windowless storerooms leading off the entrance hall. Each of these is the Venetian equivalent of one man's garden shed and it is here that wine is stored and condominium plots are hatched. Through the doors, left ajar, you can glimpse shadowy interiors, where red-faced, elderly men fix things or bottle prosecco. Where the palace gardens once stretched along the canal, there is now a small, shady courtyard.

Up until now, I have only ever seen our new flat in photographs. In those frantically busy last months before we left England, it was Alberto who had flown out to Venice to look at the place and sign for it, while I stayed behind packing and endlessly packing. Now, I push open the heavy wooden street door, and we swarm into the shadowy hall, in a flurry of heat and effort and luggage. At first, I have only a sense of dusky space; then, as my eyes adjust, I see that the hall covers most of the ground floor of the palazzo. It is flanked by two marble benches, their curlicued backs set against walls of crumbling, dirty-pink stucco. At the far end are high double doors made up of roundels of opaque Venetian glass, the skewy swirls distorting the courtyard beyond into a dim and hectic cubism. Feeling around in the gloom, I find a light switch and suddenly a wrought-iron chandelier flings the patterns of the souk around the walls. In one corner, a pair of stone lions guard the foot of the marble staircase. We marshall our forces, and begin the final haul: Lily, luggage, boys, up the four steep flights to our new home.

The apartment, like many of the properties to let in Venice, is the home of the landlord's dead mother. Pietburgo, our landlord, seems himself to be half dead: a hulking, bearded, dour-faced man, he is waiting, unsmiling, for the final signatures and the first instalment of rent.

The flat was solidly furnished in about 1950 and is, like its owner, large and awkward and gloomy. It has too much passageway and a series of odd-shaped rooms carved clumsily out of the grander fabric

22

of the medieval building. Lumpen Murano glass chandeliers hang from the ceilings and the furniture is all dark polished wood. But the flat is high up; nobody looks down on us and we, in turn, have a view across red, pantiled rooftops and bell towers. And, what is best of all, we share this eyrie with bands of skydiving swallows.

PART 2: September

Living on Water

DURING THOSE EARLY days in Venice, my sleep is threaded through with dreams of living in precipitous tower blocks, far above the ground, with a longing for trees and for the feeling of earth underfoot. I wake disgruntled and uneasy.

Lily, who has grown up in the countryside, is having nightmares and screaming herself awake, convinced that the city will be swallowed up by the great wave of a tsunami. She talks about it for days, 'What if...? What if...?' but her tsunamis ebb when I show her the long, narrow island of the Lido and tell her: 'That's what stops the big waves; it's a barrier against the sea and it makes the Lagoon.'

My own dreams take longer to go away. I feel the silence here as an absence. When I wake in the morning, only the crack of light through the shutters tells me it is time to get up; there are no other clues to help me refine that knowledge, to say whether it is 5 a.m. or 10 a.m. For the first time in my life I keep oversleeping. I miss the country birds, bantering at dawn, and the next-door chickens, roosting and fussing, then quietening, as the sun moves higher in the sky.

There are pigeons, of course, but other than in Piazza San Marco they keep a low profile. Certainly there are pockets in this city where the smaller birds chirrup, but there is hardly a teeming life of tree-dwellers, ivy-pickers, eaves-hoppers. The only constant birdcall here is the petulant shriek of gulls, those big, lone-ranging birds swooping down the canals or taking up imperious positions on chimney pots. No doubt if I can learn to understand their harsh, whee-dling conversations, they would help me out, show me where I stand in the day, the season, the year. As it is, their habits are as alien to me as those of the Venetians.

When the gulls congregate they sound like people cackling with laughter, and you could almost mistake the bleak vowels of the Venetian 'Ciao' or 'eeow', that you hear repeated all day long in the streets, for the seabirds' plaintive cries.

Sound rings differently here. Sometimes, there is a muffled quality to everything: the many walls are like full stops, cutting noise short. Or sometimes, they ricochet it back unexpectedly, so that you hear a full jazz band close by; then turn the corner and find just a couple of musi-cians in a narrow *calle*. Their modest fiddle and guitar are amplified by the surrounding buildings to something rousing and mysterious.

When I open the shutters in the morning I hear footsteps, dogs barking, cats wailing, gulls, and the heave and wash of the Lagoon as boats groan or buzz or slip along the waterways. At night, if I open the window and lean out to look along the *fondamenta* below, the silence of my closed room is all of a sudden filled with the murmur of human voices and I have the unexpected impression that I have just walked through a door, into a party.

In these early days, I find myself keenly aware, relying almost, on the cycles of the moon. At the top of this big, old building, looking out over roofs, to towers and belfries and terraces, the moon, flying high, seems the only thing left of the natural world and I follow its waxing and waning with a new attention.

The fact is, I miss my version of nature: the trees, the grass, the soil. This is when I begin to understand how visual my particular sense of the natural world is: that abundant green of the British countryside and the changes in the colour and density of vegetation that signal the changing seasons. I notice how the foliage becomes lighter or thicker or more brittle; how it begins in spring with a pale green so trans-lucently fine that it seems to vibrate; how, in the late summer sun, it works into depths of dull olive that render the landscape almost black; how, in autumn, it thins, then dries, moving through red and gold to brown. In winter, when the trees are at last bare, the blackened corpses of leaves curl into mulch, like foetal, prehistoric bog men.

These are the signs I happen to recognize. Now that they are gone and I find myself in an environment of stone, punctuated by water, I feel their absence viscerally and I can't settle. My body has to learn the new clues and how to respond instinctively to different rhythms of the natural world.

One morning, I am sitting out at the back of the *vaporetto*. The day is mild and I gaze at the passing palaces, not yet able to play the blasé Venetian and sit reading a book or staring vacantly ahead. Then, all of a sudden, there is a change; I feel it in the pores of my face. It is as if a very thin veil has drifted across the sun and the air has become heavier, softer, wetter. There is a chill, a mutedness and I remember, almost with surprise, that this city sits in the middle of the sea. What has fallen is a sea mist; here, nature is expressing itself neither with colour, nor form, but elementally, in the texture of the air, through subtle modulations of light, temperature and humidity.

On another morning, there is a monumental thunderstorm. It has been raining all night, so that as I leave the building to take the children to school, the wooden front door is difficult to shut behind us. It is swollen and distorted with water, like a drowned man. Out in the *calle*, the day is iron-grey, lights reflected in puddles and on the wet-black stone. We soon reach the bigger thoroughfare with which our street intersects. On a normal day, it is full of people, hurrying to work, university or school. The Sri Lankans who keep stalls there would usually be rigging up swathes of cheap pashminas and cheerfully crude boxer shorts, and further along the fruit and vegetable stalls would be opening for business, while the first tourists dribble in from the direction of the station. But today it is empty, except for a few solitary figures walking fast, heads down, hooded, umbrellas parrying the gusts of rain. The trinket vendors have stayed at home, the wandering holidaymakers are not tripping up the workaday folk. The weather, it seems, has given Venice back to the Venetians.

The *vaporetto* we take labours up the Grand Canal, weighed down with people who would generally be walking to work. Rain clatters on the metal roof of the boat. I look out of the steamy window and see that even at this early hour, in the grim storm-light, the empty interiors of the palaces are lavishly ablaze. Who is that person in the vast room on the *piano nobile*, with the loops of Murano chandeliers receding? It must be the Filipino woman who polishes the expanses of parquet or marble, or the Moldovan caretaker opening up.

We get off the boat and walk over the Accademia Bridge. The wood is dark and slippery. At the windy summit, my umbrella flips inside out; I wonder if anyone is ever struck by lightning in Venice.

By the time I have left the children at their school door, it has stopped raining and I decide to go home on foot. Despite the occasional spots of rain, I close my umbrella. This distinguishes me instantly as a foreigner and, most particularly, a British one; no Italian would roll up their brolley till the very last drop has fallen, upon which, they emerge, bone-dry. Italians are never damp and slightly flustered.

I walk across Campo Santa Margherita and over the bridge at San Pantalon. I have not gone much further when the rain starts again and this time it is serious. Within minutes, it is sheeting, deluging, as if a vast bucket of water is being emptied from above, at point blank range. My umbrella is useless: the rain is flying upwards from the paving stones. I stop in a doorway to wait out the storm. After a quarter of an hour, nothing has changed: the rain is coming down harder than ever and I am soaked through; I might as well keep going. I strike out across the small *campo*, wading through water. With both hands, I cling on to my umbrella which acts like the lid of a vessel, stoppered over me and submerging me in liquid. I realize that I am lost. The familiar lines and co-ordinates of the city have dissolved under the improbable quantities of water. I begin to head in what I assume to be the right direction and push down a long, narrow *calle* that does indeed bring me to the edge of the Grand Canal, but also to a dead end. I look across to my destination; short of diving into the murky depths and swimming, it is unreachable. The Grand Canal has reverted to its true nature: it is the pitching and rocking sea.

I have not seen anybody for ten minutes or more. Emptied of people, Venice gives me no indication as to whether I have been dashed ashore here in 1408 or 1608 or 1908. This underwater world is monochrome and, itself, adrift in time. The garish clutter of tourism, the thin veneer of modernity, has been washed away and all that is left is a deserted, ageing edifice, jutting out of the Adriatic. For a few hours this morning, the city has been taken back in time. Or is it forwards? One day, Venice, like Atlantis, will be engulfed by water and the fish will be its birds.

In the Giant's Castle

OUR CHILDREN WERE born and bred in England. They have the language and the culture of Britain running through their veins. But they are also half Italian and that is why we have made this decision to move to Italy, taken them from their English world and submerged them in their father's culture and language. Because five members of the family have no knowledge or experience of the system and Alberto's Italian school days ended twenty-five years ago, we are more or less starting from scratch. Inevitably, understanding school and all its ways is the biggest challenge we have in these first weeks.

The Scuola Elementare Canova, like all Venetian schools, is a forbidding building: a stone palazzo with massive double doors, heavily studded with iron bolts, which give no impression of having shed their original purpose of keeping people, aggressively, out.

On my first visit, I feel that I have walked into a giant's castle. The hall is shadowy and echoing, with a wide staircase that curves up to the first floor; the ceilings are toweringly high; the pavement, big, cold stone flags. It would be difficult to imagine a less welcoming environment for a small child arriving for his or her first day at school. If even I, a dullard adult, suspect that the grotesque, lumpen figure of the ogre's wife might crash into view at any moment, the effect on a tremulous five-year-old is unimaginable.

Fanciful as all of this may sound, there really is something of the giant's castle in the wider Italian school system. Education in this country is emphatically *not* child-centred. It is believed that each child, like Jack, fresh off his beanstalk and sneaking around the ogre's halls, must be captured and subdued by the system.

On the first day of term, a teacher marches into Michael's class at the middle school.

'I', she announces grimly to the assembled twelve-year-olds, 'have a university degree. You are still at school. You will do what I tell you because I am in charge.'

In these first few weeks of our life in Venice, I go to see one or another of my children's teachers, carrying with me a certain set of assumptions about children and education. And over and over again, I find myself sitting across the table from another adult whose ideas about children and education are not just different to my own, but diametrically opposed.

This is not always a problem and not always the case: there are many fine teachers in Italy, working their guts out on pitiful pay and against all the odds. They contend, daily, with ever more swingeing cuts. An already starving infrastructure becomes weaker and weaker. Several of these teachers are my friends and I am in awe of their selflessness and their energy in the face of such overwhelming adversity.

It seems to me that the Italian system, which is strict and dry and demanding, has some of the qualities one would have found in schools in Britain in the 1950s. There is still room for eccentrics. The legendary Raguso with his pipe in hand (sometimes, it is rumoured, lit and in his mouth) often doesn't bother with the music lessons he is meant to be teaching, but talks about morality and psychology and chess tactics and the best tobacco, and shocks and delights the kids with his dogged refusal to go by the book.

Or there is Gasparini with his unnerving wall eye, stentorian voice and famed skill in the launching of rubbers to wake up or silence inattentive students. One teacher apparently suffers from narcolepsy and falls asleep mid-sentence. I think of the old pre-Ofsted, pre-regulation days, when the British education system also polarized between teachers of pure, anarchic genius and teachers of often appalling inadequacy.

The problems arise when an already deeply inflexible system falls into the hands of angry people. At that point there is too much potential for unkindness and, on occasion, brutality. As with so much else in Italy, the situation is the opposite of what one might find in Britain.

In Britain, the current educational ethos is more or less liberal, and one of its attendant dangers is an excess of 'liberality' – in which teachers run the risk of losing their authority and control over their classes. In Italy, where the system is essentially authoritarian, the greatest danger is the reverse: that unscrupulous teachers will abuse their power over the children they teach.

This situation reflects the wider Italian culture. In a country in which individuals are often forced to survive on their wits, playing as best they can a chaotic and sometimes unfair system, there is great scope for abuse of power.

By the same count, the decent people – the intelligent and committed and humane – are often admirably vocal, and beacons of social conscience and political determination. Similarly, the Italian education system exhibits, in a very public manner, all that is best and worst in human nature.

Six-year-old Freddie has had a rocky start at school. His work has been poor, but then, one day, the class goes on a trip to a wildlife sanctuary, in a remote spot far out in the Lagoon. The children spend the morning wandering among the grassy dunes with their binoculars, searching for the little scuttling brown birds that nest there. Suddenly something lights up for Freddie and he writes a lively and enthusiastic piece about the visit. I am so happy.

At the first parents' evening, I talk with one of his teachers, Martina. She is coming to the end of her career and is in a permanent state of sour fury, like milk perpetually going off. Today, true to form, she is complaining bitterly about Freddie: his handwriting is a disaster, he doesn't listen in class but fiddles with bits of paper, he forgets everything, his homework is badly done or not done at all.

'But what about this lovely piece of writing?' I say, 'It's full of enthusiasm and good description, clear handwriting and it's two whole pages long: it's such an improvement.'

Martina looks at me coldly: 'It's on the wrong paper,' she says.

I remain calm. It is clear to me that good-natured Freddie has given up trying because Martina never gives him a scrap of encouragement or recognition. It has led to the inevitable vicious circle of poor motivation, poor performance and angry recrimination. Taking a deep breath, I go in carefully.

'I just feel – er – that if we could all – um – give him the feeling that we know he's been trying harder, he might – er – feel a bit more motivated.'

Martina's ever-unsmiling mouth turns down even further at the edges. Her voice has a peculiarly thin, harsh quality.

'Eh! And then, Signora, if I tell him he's done something well, what will he do the next day?' – she pauses, rhetorically, then gives me the definitive answer: 'Nothing!'

Her expression is one of triumph, as though she has played an unbeatable psychological trump card.

I look at Martina and realize, with despair, that she and I have exactly opposite philosophies of human nature and that there is nothing more to be said. I realize, as generations of Italians have done before me, that I'm on my own now.

Some time later Alberto and I are in the headmaster's office at Michael's school. Due to a bureaucratic error we were the only parents in his year not to have been informed of a critical last-minute change in the hours of our son's class. It has been decided that the twenty-four boys and three girls, all aged between twelve and thirteen, will have a school day that starts at 8 a.m. and goes through to 2 p.m., with a couple of ten-minute breaks, during which they will remain in the classroom.

This, it seems to me, is not merely folly, but also cruelty. All the evidence shows that children need to move in order to be able to learn; that by stimulating their bodies, you stimulate their brains. We do not want Michael to remain in this group and the school has previously assured us that they would inform us of any changes in time to move him before the start of term. There is a spare place in a parallel class because another boy has recently been moved, at his parents' request, into a different group. It seems logical that our son should take up the vacated position in that class.

We go along to the meeting relaxed and sure that we can sort it out, concerned only for Michael's well-being. Our assumption, it quickly becomes apparent, is seen by the headmaster as verging on the criminal. This man is not here for the well-being of the children; he is here to run an institution. And more than anything, he is here to win at all costs.

Serpini is a skinny little man with wire-rimmed spectacles that glint coldly. He wears over-sized and over-pressed jeans in a bid for the nonchalantly informal look. His style, it must be said, is more of a rat than a rottweiler, but when we make our request, he none the less goes, spectacularly, for the jugular, accelerating from nought to a hundred in seconds, leaning over his large desk and screeching at us, in his nasal voice, that he will not move our son under any circumstances, despite the fact that we are in this situation because of a mistake made by the school.

We have not, until now, brought up the subject of the other boy who moved classes, but under this barrage of abuse we exchange glances and Alberto pitches in:

'But headmaster, what about Luigi Pavoletti?'

'Who?' Serpini hisses, suddenly still.

'Luigi Pavoletti. His parents requested that he be moved last week and you agreed. That means there are now twenty-seven children in one class and twenty-two in the other. So doesn't it make sense to move Michael into the smaller class, into Luigi's place?'

The headmaster looks at us through his steely spectacles. His voice is tight and snide.

'I have no idea what you're talking about. How can you expect me to know what every child in this school is doing?'

I am in no doubt whatsoever that we are being shamelessly, flagrantly lied to.

'Well,' Alberto continues in an unnaturally measured tone,

'perhaps the deputy head knows something about it.' He turns to Girardini, the head's bulky sidekick in a suit, who is also present. The deputy stares back, impassive.

'I don't know what you're talking about,' he says.

The next day, determined to get justice by appealing to a higher authority than the headmaster, Alberto and I go to the Regional Education Office on the mainland. The bus rattles over the causeway, leaving the towers and canals of Venice behind. Looking out over the mudflats of the Lagoon, I think how the Venetian dream lasts only as long as you can keep it detached from reality and, most particularly, from the reality of modern Italy.

The office is in a grey concrete building in the suburbs of Mestre: the Giant's Castle in its somewhat brutalist 1970s incarnation. It is attached to a large secondary school and noisy flocks of kids are coming out of the gates as we arrive. We find our way, through endless corridors, and are, at last, shown in to see the regional co-ordinator. He does not look up as we enter, but continues to type intently. We sit down on the chairs next to his desk and wait.

The man is working among toppling heaps of documents, letters, books. His shirt sleeves are rolled up, his tie loosened, his jacket thrown over the back of the chair. He looks like a journalist in a Manhattan newspaper office, circa 1951, hunched over his clacking typewriter as he races for a deadline, tight-faced, chain-smoking. When he eventually stops typing and turns to us, his lumpy face is exhausted and unsmiling. We tell him our story.

It is immediately clear that the arrival of real parents of real children in the education office is a rare event – perhaps even unprecedented. The man is visibly irritated that we should be interrupting him as he tries so desperately to get on top of his mountainous workload. But we hold steady: we are convinced that we have a good case; that we are reasonable parents whose right it is to seek the best for their child.

After we have explained our predicament, he softens a little and concedes that what we are saying makes sense and that he will see what he can do.

'But I can't promise anything,' he warns us wearily. 'The head teacher has the ultimate power.'

A week later, we call him again.

'I think you are in the right,' he tells Alberto. 'But the head won't move on it. I'm sorry, there's nothing I can do.'

Michael continues to struggle with his difficult class and the insane hours and becomes more and more unhappy. My sense of injustice is unbearable: my son is suffering entirely unnecessarily because of the aggressive pride of someone who could so easily have helped him. The anger just won't go away.

'For the first time in my life,' I tell my friend Enrico, 'I find myself in a situation where I have an entirely reasonable case and the one person with the power to help me, refuses – out of pure, malicious pride – to do anything and then, worst of all, looks me straight in the eye and flagrantly and unashamedly lies. The sense of powerlessness is unbearable.'

Enrico smiles sadly.

'Welcome to Italy,' he says.

The Art of Arguing

I AM IN a public place – a post office, perhaps, or a sports centre or a school. There is somebody on the other side of the desk, usually a woman. The conversation goes as follows:

Me: Signora, please could you help me to ... fill out this form/pay this bill/subscribe to this service/sign my child up for this course ...

Person behind desk (unsmiling): 'Hmmm ... No ... I don't think that's going to be possible. [Silence.] Hmm ... No. No. Impossible. [Shuffles through papers.] Well, let's see. It might be possible. If you come back tomorrow at the same time, I could speak to the (boss/head teacher/ chief secretary). But I can't guarantee anything. I'll have to look for the papers and I don't know if I'll have time ...'

*

The woman behind the desk has not done her job properly unless your eventual victory feels like an anticlimactic failure. What becomes fast apparent to me is that, regardless of individual temperament, one rule reigns supreme throughout Italian officialdom: for the person behind the desk *everything* is too much trouble.

'What you have to understand about Italy,' my friend Silvia tells me, 'is that we are so frustrated and exhausted by the byzantine intricacies of our bureaucracy that the only hope we have of retaining any personal pride lies in flexing our muscles, whenever and wherever we can. If you can't beat them, you join them.'

We are sitting in the *campo* on a warm evening, drinking the Venetian aperitif Spritz; the milling people, the children playing, the soft light on the red-brick façades of the ancient buildings could not be more peaceful or harmonious.

'Either that,' Silvia adds, 'or one just gives up the fight and gets on with eating and drinking and living well from day to day, like everybody else.'

With the passing weeks, I begin to learn how to deal with people in positions of greater or lesser bureaucratic power. As with so much else there is a simple rule of thumb for a British person living in Italy: think of how you would approach the situation at home and then think of its opposite and you will have the Italian way. Whilst in Britain the notion that one is innocent until proved guilty is largely current, Italy works on the opposite principal: here, you are guilty until proven innocent. These beliefs run very deep indeed.

So, when you go into a post office and ask for a form to transfer money to pay for your child's school trip and the woman behind the counter looks at you as though you are a dangerous sex offender and speaks to you with lip-curling disdain, feel no surprise, do not weaken: STAND YOUR GROUND. Repeat the mantra: in Italy, you are guilty until proved innocent. Hold faith with the fact that in half an hour's time, after endless discussion and protracted negotiation, after much head shaking and many gloomy pronouncements that you are requesting the impossible, you are in fact very likely to achieve what you want after all – and more, so much more, the lady behind the counter will be your new best friend, and will be telling you about her mother and her varicose veins and what her son eats for breakfast.

The comedy of the quintessentially British *Fawlty Towers* lies in the fact that both Basil Fawlty *and* his hotel guests become incandescent with frustration when they do not get what they want. It is a perfect vignette of the self-righteous conviction of the British that justice *will* be done. This is the privilege of the law-givers.

Centuries of frustration in the face of power have caused a different character mutation on the Italian peninsula. Here, where there often appears to be little hope of justice, people go to operatically stylized excesses of fury – so far, so Fawlty – but then, minutes later, might ask their adversary to join them in a glass of wine, as though resigned, from the outset, to failure. I first see this when I go to our local dry cleaner with Alberto, who is, under normal circumstances, a reserved man.

He has brought with him a jacket which was marked in the cleaning process and he is determined to get his money back. Standing behind the counter is a cuboid Venetian signora with ferociously bleached and structured hair. Her heavily made-up face is a powdery brick-red. She wears a white nylon coat, with a large pale pink bow tied jauntily at her left shoulder and she stands, with both hands planted firmly on the counter, against a looped backdrop of freshly laundered sheets, like an ageing courtesan in a baroque masque. Her long nails, splayed out on the counter, are lacquered as red as a samurai helmet.

This fearsome appearance does not augur well, but Alberto explains politely to her what has happened. The signora is not, however, to be moved. It is impossible, she tells him, that this mark could have been made on her premises: clearly, the jacket was already stained when he brought it in to be cleaned.

Softly spoken Alberto is, at first, firm; he progresses to indignation and, before much longer, he is arguing fiercely. When it seems to me that the discussion can go no further, something in this mild-mannered man snaps and he undergoes a spectacular oratorical transformation. He turns his back on the woman behind the counter, lifts his jacket up high and addresses, in ringing tones, the by-now long queue of polished elderly matrons, in tweed suits, waiting to dispatch their cleaning.

'Signore!' Alberto flourishes the jacket violently. 'Signore! Would YOU bring your clothes to a dry cleaner that left them in THIS condition?!'

The matrons cluck and tut and shake their well-coiffed heads: most certainly not; never; outrageous. At which, Alberto, who knows that he has already lost the battle, bundles up his jacket and storms out of the shop. The matrons stay stolidly in line and the morning's dry cleaning business goes on.

This kind of scene is, I suppose, both good entertainment and somehow cathartic for the individuals involved. Given that in Italy there is an expectation that things will never, *ever* go your way, this theatrical integration of hopelessness into daily life must at least allow people to release a bit of the pressure.

My friend Giovanni, a professor of history, has a long-running war going with a baker whose shop is in a narrow *calle* near the university. The bakery, which has been in the same family for generations, looks like an extension of the family home, a living room eccentrically furnished with a glass counter, scales and wooden bins full of bread. There is a plasterwork Virgin Mary, a little tipsily attached to the wall, raising her hand in benediction; there are photographs of the grandchildren, a football team banner, postcards sent back from holidays around the world. Behind the counter, in a prominent position, there is also a large picture of Mussolini, glaring out at the shop and all who enter.

Every couple of months, Giovanni, who is on a mission, marches into the bakery, puffing emphatically on his cigar.

'Give me thirty rolls!' he says to the baker, an elderly, bullish-looking man, behind the counter.

Thirty rolls take up several large paper bags; slowly, the baker turns to the floury bread bins and fills the bags up, one by one. Then, he lays them on the glass counter. It is at this point that Giovanni suddenly raises both hands in dramatized horror, puffs extra hard on his cigar, and exclaims:

'Ah! But wait a minute! I have just seen that disgraceful picture of the fascist dictator displayed on your wall! I cannot possibly buy bread from you, ever again!' and stamps off the premises.

It is surprising that after a mere two months the cussed baker, a sharp-eyed Venetian who surely misses nothing, seems to have forgotten Giovanni's face and goes through the whole business of bagging up the rolls again. I understand why Giovanni continues this ritual, but what is in it for the fascist baker? A pleasure in the theatre, perhaps, or the dogged hope that this time he might just flog the goods to the troublesome lefty?

It seems to me that these apparently personal differences of opinion are markers of wider historical realities. Where Alberto sometimes appears to me unremittingly cynical about other people's motivations, I seem to him stupidly naïve in my perennial assumption of good intentions or, at the very worse, *unconsciously* bad behaviour. We are, in our small ways, re-enacting the larger, older dramas that have gone to create certain national characteristics and which, in turn – and over decades or centuries – have mulched down into individual character traits.

The Italian peninsula, where Alberto was born and bred, has seen almost two millennia of continuous political turbulence: repeated invasions by foreign powers and the fragmentation, until just over 150 years ago, into small, often warring political entities. This has created a culture that can appear to my English eyes chronically suspicious, always glancing over its shoulder in anticipation of the knife in the back. Machiavelli was, of course, a Florentine.

I, on the other hand, am the product of a country that has not been successfully invaded in a thousand years, during which time it spread itself around the entire globe, ruling and exploiting with a calm and leisurely conviction of its own righteousness. Now, the British Empire has gone, but the reach and power of the English language continues to go from strength to strength. We have a way to go yet before we feel entirely sidelined.

Is it any wonder, then, that Alberto goes for the dry-cleaning lady's jugular, while I blush with embarrassment at the brouhaha and observe, a little patronizingly, the Grand Opera of it all?

The Politics of Washing

THE PULLEY LINE extends from a hook on our building, across a court-yard, to another hook on the opposite palazzo. In order to peg out the clothes I have to lean from our fourth floor window. The ledge is at the level of my hips; this places the central point of gravity rather lower in my body than feels secure and means that hanging out the washing, that most mindless of operations, is accompanied by a nasty fluttering in the stomach, a vicious tingling in the fingertips and a distinct sense that the distribution of weight could shift at any moment so that I will topple headlong down into the bleak little walled garden of my neigh-bour, Signora Zambon. Even if I succeed in keeping my balance there is still the risk that plastic pegs, knickers and socks might slip from my hands and parachute down on to the head of the signora who has already informed me leadenly:

'The garden is mine,' as if convinced that it is only a matter of time before I storm her balding square of grass with my barbarian brood and lay claim to it.

In the early days, as I tremulously hang out clothes, then release the line a little at a time to make space for the next towel or tee-shirt, I am suddenly aware of being watched. Glancing to the right, I half jump out of my skin at the sight of an old woman, smoking intently – almost, I feel, malevolently – and staring beadily out of her window. I duck back inside as though caught in some guilty act.

A little later, I look across to another building, about 50 metres away. Clearly visible through his open window, a handsome young man in shorts lounges on his bed in the hot afternoon sun, as oblivious to me as I was to the smoking crone.

This crone, in fact, later turns out to be an invention of my own, a scrap of pure paranoia. After several months, I realize that the window where she appeared belongs, in fact, to the kitchen of our neighbour Pio and that the smoker was his by no means aged companion Alessia, a lively psychoanalyst.

Windows are bringing out the worst in me. In Venice, it is clear, you could become obsessively conscious of the scrutiny of your

39

neighbours. Either that, or develop a brazen insouciance to the gaze of other people.

The most uncomfortable overlooking of all is that of the blank window. A permanently shuttered window presents no problems: a blind, honorary wall. Windows that revealed brief moments of other people's lives are also acceptable. But there is one particular window that I can see from my sitting room that I do not like at all. It is enshrouded in a net curtain and never lit from within. This unnerves me. If anyone should happen to be looking out from behind that curtain they would see me clearly; I, on the other hand, would see nothing of them.

Glimpsed fragments of other people's lives can, though, be as comforting as a sentimental film. When I see the elegant lady across the *rio* opening the windows of her airy flat, or the family who live below her busily compressed into their few rooms – making a bed, playing the guitar, sitting in front of the computer – all seems right with the world. Surely, with so much visible, bustling, prosperous normality all around, there can be no real suffering, no tangible pain? Even the old woman I see from my dining room, who, every morning, draws her dingy net curtains and shakes out her bedding, a single light bulb suspended from the ceiling behind her, has her daily rituals and her place in my imaginative comfort zone.

But, after all, no amount of flinging open of windows or shaking out of dust is a guarantee of anything. The mystery of an apartment at the level below us is solved after months. The window is hung with a rickety Venetian blind like a lopsided mouth packed with collapsing teeth; the place appears deserted. Then, one day, as I am, yet again, hanging out the washing, I see a sick and aged man emerging on to the minute terrace like an ancient tortoise coming out from long hibernation; each step is impossibly slow so that he seems on the point of fossilizing into immobility. With one slippered foot, inch by inch, he nudges forward a plastic laundry basket. Once he and his washing have reached the outside, he begins the slow unfolding of his spine as he bends, then reaches, then takes hold of a single sock. Now, vertebra by vertebra he straightens up and moves his trembling hand towards the line upon which he intends to peg the sock. That sock could be travelling light years across the distance from basket to washing line.

I stand a pace back from the window, into the shadow. The man could not possibly see me; I am looking down on the bald crown of his head. Though I hide myself partly out of respect, and feel sorry for the extreme effort cost him by his minuscule task, I am, none the less, spying on him with unrestrained curiosity, gawping at this other life.

Meanwhile, no one else escapes scrutiny or comment. Antonio, who lives on our landing and is a big, ebullient lion of a man and a fertile source of gossip, tells me that the saturnine Signora Zambon is ragingly jealous of her equally brooding spouse.

'She's always at him,' Antonio tells me. 'She's convinced he's got hundreds of lovers. You should hear her when she gets going.'

I'm not convinced: it seems improbable to me that her husband, who has a misanthropic reluctance even to greet a neighbour on the stairs, should be engaged in extra-marital gallivanting, but Antonio is adamant. Their teenage children, he tells me, have perfectly gauged their mother's Achilles heel and can often be heard taunting the green-eyed signora for her fits of violent jealousy.

How much can one hope to conceal here, where we all live piled up, hugger-mugger? When my friend Filippo plans an illicit tryst, he arranges to meet his beloved in a bar in a distant and isolated part of the city. As they walk into the anonymous place on an anonymous street, Filippo hears a voice from behind the bar:

'Ciao! Filippo!' It is the girl who works in the bar next door to his bookshop, where he goes for coffee and brioche every morning.

'What are you doing here?' he says.

'Oh, this is my sister's brother-in-law's wife's place and I fill in for her on a Thursday afternoon sometimes.'

The fact is they could pin anything on you in Venice and, certainly, one ends up seeing the ancient Venetian predilection for masks as neither quaint nor sinister but merely desperate, and about as ineffec-tual as the act of a small child who covers both eyes with her hands and is convinced that no one can see her.

A further variation on the theme of the privacy problem is the

41

vexed question of what you do or do not hang out to dry. I, personally, draw the line at underwear and find myself prudishly protective of my own and my daughter's nightwear – this, while carelessly pegging out rows of boys' pyjamas. It occurs to me that the far from cronish, but undeniably beady-eyed, psychoanalyst who nearly scared me to death with her smoking and watching was, in fact, professionally intrigued by the psychodynamics of my laundry.

Anyway, there is no doubt that when I first arrived in September, tens of pairs of neighbourly eyes lifted washing-line-wards to clock the arrival of a large family in the long-empty Borolini apartment. And who can help but be sneakingly admiring of whoever it is who hangs out absolutely every last scrap of bra or stringy knicker on the washing line that stretches clean across the *calle* leading to the much used swimming pool and sports centre?

Now, I am putting out the washing on a soft, sunny autumn day. The unoiled pulley squeaks peevishly as I yank it along between each pegging. Our first-floor neighbour Francesco is down below in his corner of the Zambon garden (it is, it turns out, not exclusively the signora's property). He is a big, good-natured man in a washed-out blue fisherman's smock. This morning, he caught some small silver fish in the Lagoon and now, meticulously, he is cleaning his catch. I wish that my washing line wouldn't shriek so much; I want to go quietly about my business as Francesco is going about his and with at least the illusion of solitude. But, of course, at the third or fourth screech of wire rope on metal pulley, he looks up and waves, and I – pleased after all to have a genial neighbour – smile back.

The matter of washing line rights is a mystery to me. How far along one's line is it acceptable to peg the clothes? The logical answer is that since the line is mine, I should be able to peg my underwear right across to the wall of the opposite palazzo. But there are other factors to take into consideration. By doing this, I rig my laundry out over the terrace of the signora opposite. Am I therefore breaking an unwritten rule of limits, of borders, of air space Venetian style?

I decide to play safe; to heave up the flag to a horizontal half mast and, while not able to spare the signora the sight of my washing, I am at least not subjecting her to the greater indignity of taking her morning coffee, in the sunshine, with someone else's boxer shorts flapping directly overhead.

The business of space and of separation has grim shades in the Ghetto of Venice. Until the end of the Venetian Republic in 1797, it was forbidden for Jews to live outside the Ghetto, so they were forced to build not outwards but upwards, to accommodate their growing families. As a consequence, running along the side of this island within an island there is a canal where washing lines are extended palazzo to palazzo, far higher over the water than in the rest of the city.

On these distant, high-strung wires, lanky trousers and diaphanous shirts swell and flap in the wind with a particular, far-away beauty, like balloons escaping into the blue. In the sometimes comically public world of this city, it seems that the public washing of one's linen can achieve a kind of poetry if only because a section of the population, with ample reason to reach, metaphorically speaking, for masks or to acknowledge paranoia with pragmatism, were forced to go skywards and had to hang out their washing accordingly.

Authentic

WITHIN WEEKS OF my arrival in the Calle del Vin, the landscape of the street has changed. First, the kindly, harassed, grey-haired woman who runs the stationery shop at the end of the street announces that she is closing down her business in order to move closer to her grandchildren, on the mainland.

A month later, the crowded little shop, which is always cheerfully packed with schoolchildren stocking up on the inordinate quantities of stationery devoured by the Italian school system, is empty.

It is not long before a young Chinese man is to be seen at a lone desk, in the otherwise bare premises. A few Perspex photo frames have been placed in the window along with a sign explaining that he will frame photographs on order. His wife, with a baby on her hip, appears occasionally.

Soon after that, an antiquated haberdasher's shop halfway up the *calle* announces its intention to close with a small, handwritten card in the window. The place smells of old fabric and old cardboard and behind the counter there sits a quiet, smiling, plainly dressed girl whom I imagine to be the proprietor's granddaughter. The dozens of little wooden drawers full of buttons and pins and threads must have been stocked years before her birth.

Both of these events inspire in me a feeling of anxiety – panic even – a sense that no sooner have I arrived in Venice than the last, precious scraps of real Venetian-ness are disappearing before my very eyes. Thank God, I think, that the second haberdasher's shop, at the other end of the *calle*, is still there. But even this cannot last and before another month has passed, brown paper has been taped all over the insides of those windows too, and one more fragile, indigenous light has been snuffed out.

Filled with the gloomy conviction that I have, as it were, arrived a day late for the party, I begin to notice just how many shut-up premises there are in the city. And how many of those that are still open sell one of four commodities: pizza, ice cream, glass or masks. This is when I begin to ask myself what it is, precisely, that I want of this place?

The fact is that I want – crave even – an 'authentic' Venice, where 'real' Venetians live 'real' lives. And what, after all, is that?

In Venice, you often hear a statement prefaced with the words '… as a Venetian …' or '… we Venetians …' Monica wants to move house and tells me about an apartment she has been to see.

'But you know,' she shrugs, 'It was no good. As a Venetian, when I went in, I didn't feel as though I was in Venice.'

What could this mean? Certainly something very different from what an American, for example, might have in mind when he says: 'as an American …'

The catch-all prefix connects the individual American to an abstract national ideal, but this is not what my Venetian friend is expressing. She is using her group identity to express a condition of belonging physically, even aesthetically, to her city. While an American might bear his American-ness before him wherever he goes in the world, like a passport, or a sheriff's badge, a Venetian's sense of shared identity is so much linked to the actual place that it evaporates the minute he or she leaves the collection of tiny islands that is home, and sets foot on *terraferma*.

Announcing yourself as American could be seen as an act of assertion; it may even be felt as imperialism. But Venice's imperial days are long gone, and to appeal to Venetian-ness is now the diametric opposite of imperialism: it is a proud and desperate attempt at survival by a people, whose island home is constantly, daily, invaded by millions of strangers with no real investment in the place.

One evening, we join a group of parents and children from the elementary school for a start-of-year pizza in Campo Santa Margherita. The September night is balmy and we parents sit out at tables while our children swarm over the well at its centre, or play football. As we chat, Flavia, one of the mothers, suddenly breaks off in mid-sentence, stands up abruptly and strides across the *campo*. A young tourist is photographing some of our children as they clamber over the antique well and Flavia collars him furiously, telling him that he has no right to take pictures of children without their parents' permission. He retreats, visibly confused.

'We've become part of the sideshow,' Flavia storms, as she sits back down at the table.

Venetians are not going down without a fight. This small community is full of groups and committees promoting local events and activities. There are youth groups, community groups, dance companies, theatre companies, choirs, rowing clubs. There are associations working for residents to change policy on housing, transport, the environment.

Events that come from outside are also, of course, part of the real life of the city. The rich influx of the arts is enthusiastically embraced by many of the people who live here; the Biennale exhibitions, visiting speakers, concerts, opera and theatre are all part of the lives of

Venetians. But the difference between Venice and any other city, the reason why there is so much sensitivity and debate about what is and is not Venetian, lies in the uniquely critical problem of numbers. The citizens of Venice are so vastly outnumbered by the visitors to Venice that there is no balanced relationship between the city and the world at large. There is no equal exchange in which the city offers up her history and her beauty in return for the cultural riches brought in from the outside world. Not surprisingly, this leads to a deeply ambivalent, not to say confused, reaction to outsiders.

As a foreign resident, I encounter this ambivalence daily. I am neither one thing nor the other in the eyes of many 'true' Venetians and I am as likely to find myself disgracefully overcharged in a bar and treated with casual disdain by the waiter as I am to be treated with charm and courtesy.

I have been learning how to *voga*, or row in the traditional Venetian style, which is to say, standing up like a gondolier. One day, for the first time, I row up the Grand Canal with my friend Jane. She is steering at the back and I am at the front of her old lagoon craft, a Coda di Gamba, or prawn tail. It would be impossible to say how many times we are photographed in the twenty minutes it takes us to get from Ca' d'Oro to the Salute. Those tens of people clamouring to record their Venetian experience can have no idea that their subjects are an English and Australian woman, navigating their boat, much, it must be said, to the general hilarity of the *gondolieri*, taxi boat drivers, delivery-boat men and other, assorted, 'real' Venetians, who call out to us good-humouredly as we make our zig-zaggy path between the palaces.

So what is it we are after when we hunt for the 'authentic'? The very notion of the real or genuine – the original – is problematic where Venice is concerned; how could there ever have been a truly aboriginal inhabitant in this particular Garden of Eden – an artificial construction on water, an historic meeting place between east and west, in a millennial flux of trade and war?

'Ha!' snorts Giovanni, the historian, 'True Venetians? There are

FIVE of them!'

'Ah yes, dialect ...' Donatella thinks carefully for a moment. Then, eyes lighting up, hand poised. 'Yes, I know! The best speaker of dialect is Alvise's brother's wife's mother-in-law.'

This is a city where even the locals have to peer hard to find the genuine article and then, the very last of their race, they count them on the fingers of one hand.

And what, after all, is this authentic Venice?

Walking along a back canal on a soft, sunny September morning, heading for a market no tourist will ever see unless they have got really, chronically lost, I pass two men sitting on the *fondamenta* on upturned oil cans.

One of them is large, black-bearded and piratical; the other is small, with a typically wiry Venetian build. They are talking with animation in the thick, consonantal, sometimes nasal Venetian dialect that is so far from the pretty, lilting melodies of Italian. As they bellow amiably at each other, the pirate is sorting deftly through a stream of hundreds of very small crabs scuttling and slipping down a long, metal tray that he has balanced across his knees. The other man is untangling a matted bunch of fishing nets.

How delighted I am to have come upon this scene! How senti-mentally gratified! Hungry, as I am, for proof that I have not, after all, arrived in Venice too late to witness and perhaps even participate in its Real Life, these two men seem heaven sent: Real Venetians, doing Real Venetian Things.

Not long after this, I am out with a friend, strolling peaceably among the pines at the outer edge of the city, while her dog pursues invisible sniffing trails through the mangy grass and stops intensely at the foot of trees or lamp posts.

A little way from us, there is a short, fat old woman, with an equally short and fat dog, of uncertain provenance, which proceeds to poo abundantly in the middle of the path. The woman seems not to register the steaming heap her dog has deposited, and waddles on.

'Signora!' calls out my friend. 'Your dog –' she smiles and points. The old woman turns on us with a look of undiluted contempt, her pencilled orange eyebrows riding high into her sparse, candy-floss hairline, her scarlet lips pursed with pantomime dame disdain.

'I,' she says, 'live here.'

'So do I,' replies my Scottish friend, 'and I think it's important that we clean up after our dogs – there are lots of children playing in the park.'

'I,' spits the old woman definitively, 'have lived here for seventy-four years.'

When my sons come home from school they take the *vaporetto* to ferry them across the Grand Canal. One afternoon, they get on a Number Three, the short-lived line introduced for residents only. They show the *marinaio* their season tickets to prove that they live in the city and then stand by the rail and chat together in English for the few minutes of the crossing. This is when an aged woman approaches the *marinaio* and hisses loudly:

'Those three – they're not Venetians!'

The *marinaio* shrugs, 'I've seen their passes.'

But mere residency never satisfied the true racist.

Everyone in Venice is, it seems, engaged in the debate about what is authentically Venetian and, given the numbers of visitors, it is hardly surprising that certain sections of the population are no longer able to distinguish between the valuable and the destructive when it comes to newcomers. Older Venetians mourn the passing of the Venice of their youth, where children played out in every *calle* and communities were strong. Yet those three half-Italian boys, rucksacks on their backs, travelling home from school, are not enough for the woman on the *vaporetto* because they were not born Venetians.

At first sight, it seems extraordinary that in one of the most visited metropolises in the world there still exist people who cannot, *will* not, conceive of a community which could encompass both an 'indigenous' and an immigrant population. But, of course, it is precisely because Venice is so incessantly tramped over, so repeatedly used for one purpose only – the passing gratification of its visitors – that some 'real' Venetians have closed down and switched off.

Has this largely unregulated mono-economy destroyed Venice once and for all – leaving a monument that is indubitably more attractive, but no less dead, than any other burnt-out place, where a few last natives still hobble around, forever uselessly debating who is really Venetian?

Sacca Fisola is a residential area that sits at the end of the large island of the Giudecca. All the cruise ships that go through the city pass by there.

In April, I am sitting on the *vaporetto* heading towards the Sacca and see that somebody has draped a vast banner across the trees growing along the edge of the water. It reads:

NO ALLE CROCIERE!
(No to cruise ships!)

This is a protest against the damage caused by the liners that blunder daily up and down the Giudecca Canal. These monstrously large floating hotels threaten environmental devastation to the city and to the ecosystem of the Lagoon. They disgorge more than a million people every year, who then flood through Venice for an hour or two, leaving their rubbish, clogging the narrow streets, and bringing little benefit to the local traders, beyond the purchase of a few souvenirs or the odd bottle of water.

The banners could not be better positioned. The pinprick figures lining the decks, listening to the booming guided commentaries, watching the pinnacles of the fabled city passing by, can easily make out the big red letters. But there is one problem: how many of those people can read Italian?

Around the same time, the newspapers publish an extraordinary photograph taken in quite another part of the planet. The picture has been shot from an aeroplane flying low over the Amazon jungle. Below, in a forest clearing, there is a group of naked men, daubed in bright red paint. They are standing among grass huts and are shooting up at the aircraft with bows and arrows. They are, the caption explains, members of a tribe that has never before had contact with modern society. Desperately trying to ward off these intruders from the sky, their arrows are not even touching the side of the plane.

This is all part of an ancient debate about the Authentic, a conversation as revealing of cultural anxiety – Who am I? Where do I belong? – as it is of cultural breakdown. And, of course, the question of what is or is not authentic will inevitably come to a head at times and in places where the 'authentic' status quo seems to be radically threatened. In a climate of political, economic or spiritual uncertainty people crave safety, and what could be safer than the past: a place of origins, of fixed values and predictable outcomes? Arcadia always was a heavenly place.

Globalization and the right to, and possibility of, unlimited access (both of which are central to most tourism) run radically counter to the local, the private, the traditional. It occurs to me that those two fishermen, chatting in the sun on the *fondamenta*, might begin to appear as precious, as rare and as doomed as the Red Men of Amazonia.

Meanwhile, back in the Calle del Vin, new developments are underway. The young Chinese man, who has tried without success to fish in the stream of the passing tourist trade with his Perspex photo frames, has decided on another strategy: he has reinvented the wheel and is filling his shop with pens, reams of paper, files and folders, until it is as stuffed with stationery as ever before and the local students and schoolchildren are beginning to go back there again for their supplies.

Shortly before Christmas, to my great relief, the brown paper on the windows of the haberdasher's shop at the end of our *calle* comes down and a gorgeous fantasia of haberdashery is revealed: looped swathes of satin ribbons in pink and purple; balls of emerald and sky blue cashmere heaped in pyramids; scatterings of fabric roses, tumbling-forward rolls of shimmering gold velvet. And in the place of the bent old woman, in her fawn knits and slippers, who once fussed and shuffled behind the counter, is a slender and beautiful young woman who might have belonged to another species altogether, except that she sweeps and scrubs the shop's stone threshold as obsessively as any other Venetian matron before her.

At about the same time, halfway up the *calle* in the other direction, the shy, plain haberdasher's granddaughter emerges from her chrysalis. The cotton reels and buttons, it is true, have been consigned to history, but the granddaughter has not. Sounds of sawing and drilling begin to come from the boarded shop. Something is up. At last, after several weeks of noisy activity, all is revealed: a poster in the window announces the opening of her new clothes shop. On the first day of the new enterprise, the haberdasher's granddaughter is wearing tight jeans and vertiginous stilettos; her face is brighter and bigger with make-up. In the shop window, headless female dummies sport plunge-neck tops and gold-trimmed mini-skirts, while their muscular, plasticated male counterparts appear in cap-sleeved tee-shirts with slogans like 'Hollywood Look' or 'James Dean Bikers Academy' emblazoned across their ample chests.

The opening of this shop is a triumph for 'authentic' Venice, though it is doubtful that any tourists will ever take a picture of the haberdasher's granddaughter's window display. The clothes she is selling are the preferred uniform of a certain section of 'indigenous' Venetian society. It seems likely that her new business will thrive, since the *calli* and *fondamente* nearby teem with people sporting exactly this style of dress. Just metres off one of the main tourist drags, the Real Venice has fought back and, for now at least, it has won.

Meanwhile, like a large and unlikely decoy duck, I will continue to row up and down the Grand Canal and be, extravagantly, photographed.

PART 3: October

Hospitality

IT IS A warm autumn afternoon, and we are sitting in the sun outside a bar, by a canal. Roland has brought his new skateboard; he is already very good and goes on it to school every day. He has, rather brilliantly, mastered the technique of reading a book at the same time: his eyes are fixed intently on the page as, with minute knee and ankle bends and fluid hip movements, he weaves a sinuous path among the oncoming pedestrians.

Today, as Alberto and I sit drinking hot chocolate, Roland is practising flips and swerves on the wide *fondamenta* outside the café. Then, suddenly, the board slips from between his feet and shoots, like a pea popping from its pod, towards the canal. Roland, who is lithe and quick, is after it in a moment, but the board is faster than he is and it tips over the edge, elegantly, like an acrobat executing a back flip. Roland vaults down from the *fondamenta* into a small, wooden boat moored there, but he lands just a second too late, in time only to see the skateboard slide silently to the muddy bottom of the canal.

Roland, however, is not silent; he has fallen badly and is crying with the pain. Alberto pulls the sobbing child on to his shoulders and we head for the hospital.

Venice's hospital – L'Ospedale Civico di Santi Giovanni e Paolo – is the most eccentrically beautiful building I know. The top of the

marble façade is like a lopsided crown of delicately descending scal-
lops, beneath which are grand but curiously squashed trompe l'oeuil
columns, and lions set in bizarre perspectives, all of which gives the
impression of many things going on, but mostly out of sight, just
around the corner.

The great entrance courtyard is a sea of ancient and perilously
undulating pavement, punctuated by stone pillars. For centuries,
people have been coming here for the same continuous purpose. But
putting history and aesthetics aside, it strikes me how very difficult it
must be for the halt and the lame to navigate a safe passage across this
space: it would be hard to imagine anything much further from the
ideal image of a modern hospital.

Now, with Roland hanging on to Alberto's back in grimly stoical
silence, we follow a surreal route of impersonal hospital corridors
that morph unexpectedly into renaissance courtyards or arcades and
then back again into hospital corridors, until we eventually arrive in
casualty. We present ourselves at the reception desk and finally take
our place on plastic chairs, along with all the other minor medical
flotsam and jetsam cast up by this particular Venetian afternoon. We
settle down to wait.

After an hour, I revise my opinion of the Ospedale Civico. Casualty,
whether it is housed in a stupendous renaissance building in the
middle of the Venetian Lagoon or in a jerry-built cottage hospital in
the Midlands, is the same the world over: a place of infinite general
boredom, punctuated by the odd high-octane drama, set off either
by mental imbalance, pain or frustration. It is the *Divine Comedy*
rewritten for the twenty-first century: the circles of Hell and Heaven
have merged, for the most part, into a single zone: medical purgatory,
with its rows of chairs and endlessly waiting people. Death and Mercy
make their incursions, of course, but casualty is, at its heart, the no
man's land of a world that prefers to ignore the existence of both.

When eventually Roland's ankle is x-rayed, it is found to be
broken. We wait for another long time to have it plastered up. When
we emerge from the hospital, it is 8 p.m. and dark. There is an ambu-
lance boat that does the rounds of the city every few hours, dropping

people near to their homes, but we have just missed the last one and the next will not leave until after midnight. We decide, just this once, to take a water taxi, and approach one waiting near to the hospital entrance.

'Calle del Vin,' says Alberto, to the handsome, tanned young man in pressed white jeans, a leather jacket and designer stubble standing at the wheel. 'How much?'

'A hundred and twenty.'

We are speechless. We could walk there in ten minutes. If we could walk.

'But it takes five minutes to get there by boat! And our son has broken his ankle.'

Skinny little Roland on his crutches looks like something out of Dickens, shivering forlornly in the chill night. The taxi driver shrugs.

'All right then. A hundred.'

We are over a barrel. After much haggling, we get it down to eighty euros. It is, metre for metre, without doubt the most expensive trip we have ever made. The Venetian taxi driver, pouting all the way to the bank, has taken his pound of the foreigner's flesh.

Unlearning IKEA

It is a drear autumn day soon after our arrival and I am hurrying across a small, grey *campo* in the rain. An old woman is leaning against the stone portal of a building, a carrier bag of shopping slumped at her feet. She is tightly wrapped in a wool coat; her legs are so terribly thin that her thick beige nylon tights sag at her ankles; she has the gaunt fragility of extreme age, but her voice is strong when she calls out to me.

'Signora, excuse me, but could I ask you to take my bag up the stairs and leave it outside my door?'

In twenty brief seconds I run up the short flight to the first floor and leave the shopping propped against the wall.

'Thank you, Signora, thank you so much.'

Very, very slowly, she turns and begins to mount the first step, grasping the stair rail with both hands. Her face is strained with the effort, but she pauses to smile back at me over her shoulder.

'I can get up if I hold on like this, but I can't manage the bag at the same time. Thank you again. Some days I have to wait for half an hour for somebody to go by.'

Measured against modern ideas of convenience, Venice can be wildly impractical and often uncomfortable. If you have no access to a private boat or are hampered physically in any way (age, disability, luggage, babies), or simply do not have a lift in your building, the logistics of daily life can range from the tricky to the nightmarish. But there is another side to this: physical restrictions that might at first seem limiting, even to the able-bodied, enforce a speed and rhythm of living that is on an entirely human scale. The 4x4 that I park outside the supermarket is a sagging blue shopping trolley; the 'supermarket', as often as not, is the greengrocer's stall on the corner of the street, the sweet-smelling cubby hole of a bakery, the butcher or the fishmonger. The £200 bumper shop at the out-of-town Megastore, complete with desert wastes of car park, clattery, disobedient metal trolleys, bulging excrescences of plastic bags, aisle after neon aisle of hammering choice, choice, choice, has shrunk to five minutes on the way home: a brief, friendly transaction with someone you see every day and the purchasing of ingredients for one meal – or perhaps two.

During my first months in the city I unfailingly buy too much food and end up hauling splitting bag-loads of groceries up the four flights of stairs to our apartment. Finally, though, I get it and begin to purchase just enough and no more. That is when I stop even noticing the shopping. It becomes an organic, practically invisible part of the walk back from school. Everything is scaled down: individual serves individual; bread and fruit and vegetables are mostly sold in paper bags and a plastic carrier doubles as tomorrow's rubbish container. The physical constraints imposed by the city mean that daily life unfolds in a sustainable, human dimension. I am beginning to understand that in Venice, you can, quite simply, go no further than it is possible to walk (with a little help from the plodding *vaporetti*) and you can never transport more than you can carry.

This is why IKEA in Padua represents a kind of consumer nemesis for inhabitants of Venice. Back on the mainland, I revert immediately to being a citizen of the modern world of hyper mobility. Once the car has been parked and I am inside that great corrugated-iron box of a selling machine, ambling obediently along the yellow brick road of tape, through the forests of sofas and shelves, chairs and tables, lampshades and glasses and cushion covers, all memory of the necessary minimalism of life in Venice magically disappears.

This is why, some hours later, I find myself back at Piazzale Roma with a vast and weighty flat pack balanced on my trolley, which I must now get home by heaving it up and down bridges and manouvring it around corners, with the strain on my lower back proving quite possibly terminal.

Or I may find that it is raining and that the several enormous brown paper bags, full of candles and nests of Tupperware that I had not known I wanted, are fast turning to papier-mâche. The once bright plastic drops out of the sodden bottom into a muddy puddle and I am still half an hour's walk from home. The shining, the new, the practically free, suddenly feels less alluring; may even start to look like folly.

Self-service

> *'Nel mezzo del camin di nostra vita mi ritrovai per una selva oscura che la diritta via era smarrita.'*

> ('Midway on life's journey, I went astray
> from the straight road and found myself
> alone in a dark wood.')

THE GREENGROCER OVER the bridge from whom I buy my fruit and vegetables is fighting a one-man battle for Venice and the values of his Venetian culture. Giuseppe has a prime position on a busy Venetian thoroughfare. Every morning he displays his produce outside his shop:

a handsome stack of apples and pears, aubergine, cabbages, artichokes, plums and bananas and leeks. The greengrocer is a sad, decent, angry man.

'I was a bank manager for twenty years,' he tells me. 'I belonged to the ultra left. Then, one day, I turned on the path, to look behind me and I saw that there was no one there. So I thought: better to spend the rest of your life selling fruit and vegetables than this.'

He smiles grimly, baring his nicotine-stained teeth.

As we talk, he glances over my shoulder every so often at the produce displayed outside his shop. Then, suddenly, he shoots past me and out on to the street.

'NO SELF SERVICE!' he barks harshly at a drifty blond American girl half submerged by her rucksack, who has picked up a peach and is turning it around to see whether or not it is ripe. She does not understand.

'No self service!'

'No?' she says wonderingly, thinking, it seems, that this irate foreign shopkeeper is telling her that she is not allowed to buy from his gorgeously laden stall. She is clearly confused, but accepting the prohibition as though it had some obscure Alice in Wonderland logic, she drifts away again.

Giuseppe comes back into his shop.

'I am sorry, Signora,' he says, apologetic and shaken by his own fury. 'These people cannot behave in this way. Would you go into someone's house and finger their food and then just put it down and leave again?'

'No, of course not,' I say, because from that point of view his logic is impeccable. 'But they simply have no idea that picking up the fruit and touching it is unacceptable. That's what you do where they come from.'

Giuseppe will not understand; cannot understand.

When I go to Giuseppe to buy an avocado or some peaches, he will say:

'Is it for tonight?' and I might reply, 'No, some time over the next few days would be fine.'

And because the fruit I want is still firm, he will sell it to me. If I need it that day, he does not sell it to me. I do not need to finger and bruise his peaches – he knows exactly how ripe they are and will tell me. He is always right and he has a relationship with his customers based on trust and his knowledge of what he is selling. To tell them anything except the truth about what they are buying would be to shoot himself in the foot – unhappy shoppers take their custom elsewhere. These are human-scale relationships of mutual convenience that work.

When the foreigners trek past his shop in what Giuseppe sees as a sort of cultural breaking and entering – part of tourism's systematic rape of his city – he does not, it strikes me, really see them as human. The American girl has floated in from the land of infinite supermarket aisles, where the only non-shopping human beings are the armies of shelf-stackers, who probably know nothing about the produce they are handling. She is no better equipped than Giuseppe to understand another point of view.

One might see this America of uncontrolled and self-spawning consumerism as itself a kind of victim – a poor little rich country. But for Giuseppe, keeping guard over his vegetables, American culture is only the enemy.

Do Not Disturb

'LILY', STEFANIA INFORMS me, 'is azure.'

I look at my small daughter, who is still, in these early days at school, leaning on her zimmer frame.

'She has a special soul, she's different from the others.' Stefania explains, 'I thought you would know. You've got all those crystals.'

She nods at my necklace and rings. I look down in surprise; I hadn't realized they gave so much away.

'You don't see these azure children very often,' she adds knowingly.

Stefania, whose family, she tells me, is Venetian from way back, looks more like a native American. She is in her early fifties and rather large, with very long, jet black hair, a wide face and a straight nose. She, herself, is swathed in necklaces, rings and bangles and is wearing a voluminous tie-dyed kaftan top. She has an air of kindly indolence that extends to her teaching practice, which, according to Lily and Roland, entails doing not very much at all. Unless, that is, events turn to her real, alternative area of expertise.

When Lily tells her she is not feeling well, Stefania moves swiftly into action. She lays both hands on the child's head and breathes deeply through her nose several times. Then, she lifts her right hand and draws it slowly away from Lily, extending her arm as far as she can from her body, at which point she vigorously shakes her hand, as though shaking raindrops off her fingertips. Then, she lifts her left hand and does the same thing. She appears to be pulling something out of Lily's head and casting it away. Her eyes are closed in intense concentration and she sways slightly. This goes on for some minutes, with alternating hands. Eventually, she stops.

'Now,' Stefania murmers, looking Lily deep in the eyes. 'Do you feel better?'

'No,' says Lily.

At the end of the school day, Stefania comes out of the door with the children, leans up against the wall and lights a cigarette, which she proceeds to smoke, with long, slow drags. I imagine the effect this would have outside our village school in England and smile. But Stefania's lungs are demanding in other ways too and these amuse me less.

Behind the elementary school there is a wonderful park, with huge plane trees and grassy knolls: a kind of paradise for these Venetian kids who are so bound in by stone walls and mostly live in small, gardenless flats. But Stefania rarely takes the class outside at break time. She is allergic to the trees, she tells us, so the seventeen lively nine-year-olds, who have sat through two hours of lessons already, simply have to stay inside. At first, they are allowed to play in the hallway, but they are judged to be too unruly and end up in the classroom for five hours at a stretch.

Stefania's refusal to give these children exercise is entirely sanctioned by the system. Many of the teachers do not take the children out – it's too far to go all the way down those stairs for such a short break; it's too wet, too hot, too windy, too dusty; the children will catch cold; the children have been too naughty. There's always some excuse. So the kids continue to gaze, like Alice, out at the unobtainable garden and the teachers continue to complain vociferously to the parents that their children are wild, uncontainable and incorrigibly fidgety.

Venetian children get used to the physical constraints, both necessary and unnecessary, of their city and culture. In our first months here, I am acutely aware of the impact my family of non-Venetians has on the world around them. Four children brought up in the English countryside are altogether louder and more numerous than the average Venetian family of one or two children. Lily, Michael, Roland and Freddie have grown up without having to think about the people downstairs or upstairs; they are used to having space and to filling it, with their gestures and their voices and their belongings. Every morning, we tumble out of our building and into Calle del Vin and it is as if the circus has arrived in town.

But it's not only the numbers and the volume that makes us so very conspicuous, it's our style: the hastily brushed hair, the unbuttoned and brightly coloured coats, the continuing argument or the loud pleas for a snack from the cake shop. The twins, who are in the middle of a knitting craze, sit at the back of the *vaporetto* and knit their way up and down the Grand Canal, like a couple of old ladies and I, who love nothing more than being an invisible observer, must submit to being a beacon of foreignness as I roll across town with my gaggle of kids.

When Venetian children come out of school, they head with their parents, grandparents or au pairs for the *campo*. These public spaces are the playgrounds of Venice. Adults stand in clusters chatting and their children race around them until darkness begins to fall and then, because this is Italy, everyone goes in for dinner at the same time.

Often, standing in the *campo*, I think of that Breughel painting of children playing in a sixteenth-century Flemish square – scuffling,

tumbling, pretending, competing – dozens of kids exuberantly occu-
pying their public space. And here they are still: kicking and throwing
balls, chalking pictures on the flagstones, hopscotching, giggling, skip-
ping, eating ice creams, scootering and skateboarding.

After school, I am chatting with some of the other mothers as
our children roar about in the *campo*, letting off steam after the long
school day, when a sweet-faced elderly American woman engages me
in conversation. She is in Venice for two reasons. Not many years ago,
when they were staying in the city, her husband died suddenly and
unexpectedly, and now she has returned to this place of loss and her
last happiness. But besides that, she is also here to continue, alone, the
sociological and architectural studies they carried out together for
years:

'Our conviction was that we needed to develop in America a
consciousness of the public space as a valuable and creative facility. A
place where you are on foot, not insulated in your car; where you can
stop and talk, play, eat and drink, look around you, be together with
other people, some of whom you know, some of whom are strangers.'

There is something touchingly solitary about her as she gestures
around this very communal space, heaving with people of all ages.

'This,' she smiles warmly, 'is good.'

But, of course, the street life of Venice isn't all roses and the same
battles continue to be waged between the old and the young.

Just outside our house, there is a *rio terà* or filled-in canal. This
creates a wider than normal area in this city of narrow byways and is
perfect for football and other games. According to people who have
lived here all their lives, this particular *rio terà* was once full of kids
careering up and down after balls, all of which culminated every so
often in legendary mass football games wildly played out between the
youths of the neighbouring parishes.

When we first move in, the *rio terà* is taken up with building works
and, except for a few people passing through, it is deserted. But the
arrival of four new kids on the block and, at the same time, the end of
the works means that it soon begins to fill up again. Every day, after
school, a band of boys that includes Freddie and Roland play football

there. Huddles of girls and younger children play less rumbustious games happily around the edges.

But no authentic Venetian street scene would be complete without its grumpy old men and women. So, perfectly on cue, the elderly couple on the top floor of the building opposite begin to grumble and complain.

'You can't play out there between 1 o'clock and 4 o'clock,' they snap at the children. 'You can only play in the street between 4 and 6.'

This injunction is cordially ignored, but the children, it is clear, are becoming the focus of intense resentment.

'You've broken my front door with your football,' the old woman tells the boys bitterly. Given that the door is a great, weighty wooden thing studded with metal and designed hundreds of years ago to resist much more threatening foes than a plastic football bought for a euro at the newsagents, I remain sceptical, but understand that the real problem is not structural.

Then, one day, the old woman's husband comes out and says menacingly to the careening footballers, 'We're watching you! We know where you live!'

Which strikes us as not especially brilliant, given that we live in the house opposite. Anyway, despite repeated threats to call the *carabinieri*, the *carabinieri* never come.

This is par for the course. Visitors to Venice are mostly blithely unaware of the seething, muttering Venetians on the *vaporetti* who are cursing them audibly for cluttering up their streets and their boats and for having the gall to be there at all.

Though I dislike the rudeness, I do understand: the Venetians are drowning in tourism. What, on the other hand, I cannot comprehend is the venom they direct towards the children of the city, who are, after all, their own kind and the only hope that Venice has of one day becoming again a place for the people who live here and not a mere temporary staging post for millions of tourists.

Often, older Venetians speak lovingly and sadly of the days when the city was properly, fully inhabited. Another of our neighbours, a kindly, elegant man in his seventies, recalls how, when he was a small boy, the children had long-jumping contests off the well in the nearby *campo*: a kind of impromptu, Venetian juvenile Olympics. He remembers perilous swimming races across the Giudecca Canal and the kids dive-bombing off the bridges, when the summer heat became unbearable.

My friend Roberta, who is in her forties, tells me how she and her friends would race home from school on boats, leaping along the canal from craft to craft, with a weather eye for the owners, who would sometimes catch them and give them a furious rocketing.

The city is painfully aware of the loss of a younger generation. Years before, on a visit to Venice, we were walking along a wide *fondamenta* with all four of our then very small children strung out like ducklings behind. A tiny, bent and ancient woman stopped to watch as we went by.

'Signora!' she said, her eyes shining in her frail, wrinkled face. 'Are they all yours?! It's like a fairy tale!'

She seemed to be returning to a folk memory, to a time when families were very big indeed – a time, in fact, when a family of four children would have been on the small side. Now, in these melancholy days of a chronically falling national birthrate, it felt to her like a miracle.

And yet and yet … the living children, the children of now, are, when they actually begin to play in the actual street, just too much trouble. It's a predictable enough story – how youthful energy, youthful noise, can be exhausting and somehow cruel to the old: a heartless flouting of age and its unjust ills. All the same, it has a pathetic irony in this fatally depopulated city that is so desperately in need of youthful, resident blood.

One afternoon, when I am letting myself into our house, while the kids of the neighbourhood play noisily around me, the young man who looks after the small hotel opposite approaches me nervously.

'Signora,' he is visibly embarrassed, but clearly there is something he has to say. 'Couldn't the children play a little further up there?' He points miserably towards the end of the *rio terà*. 'You see, they might disturb the tourists.'

The Last Laugh

ADRIANA IS WEARING a hairband to which are attached a pair of green Shrek ears. This does nothing to reduce her impact. On Adriana, even Shrek's ears assume a look of authority and of the unavoidable. She is one of Freddie's teachers, and Freddie, himself the beau ideal of stubbornness, has met in Adriana his match and nemesis.

'There's a group of foreign mothers,' she tells me, 'which meets a few times over the winter and everyone brings something – a recipe or a song, perhaps – from their own culture and they make a lovely book and bring it into schools and dress up in their national costumes and talk about their countries with the children.'

Adriana is a force of nature and hard to resist.

'Yes,' I say, entering into her enthusiasm, 'and there are so many foreign parents at this school that you must have a real goldmine to draw on – '

But I see, in the minute flicker of Adriana's face muscles, that I am missing the point. The charming Irish glass designer, the clever Parisian translator, the chic German costumier, the Polish archeologist and the Russian painter who gather outside the school to wait for their children are not the kind of foreign mothers the Foreign Mothers' Group is after. The sort of foreign mothers required are the really foreign kind, not educated, bilingual European women, but recently arrived immigrants from hotter, poorer, farther away places. It occurs to me that I, fresh from an English village, reasonably fluent in Italian and working for Radio Four, might not entirely meet Adriana's criteria. Still, I understand, that as the newest foreign mother in town, she needs me to meet her quota. Obediently, I go along.

The meeting is to take place in yet another lowering palazzo turned primary school. The outside of the building is made of great blocks of rough stone and is windowless at ground floor level; the doors are heavily studded and have many enormous keyholes.

I step up on to the stone threshold and press the bell – the nose of a bronze lion.

'Who is it?' comes a disembodied voice from the door phone.

'I'm here for the Foreign Mothers' Group.'

The door clicks open and I go through into the deserted entrance hall.

I stand in the semi gloom for some moments, wondering where I should go. There is no one in sight. Then, somewhere deeper in the building, I hear a distant echo of voices and so I follow the sound until I come to another double door that stands slightly ajar. I peer through into the poorly lit depths of a hall. There are stacks of tables and chairs, and large objects – blackboards, perhaps – draped in sheets. I have the impression of being in an abandoned furniture depository. At one end of the room is a stage, around which are rigged heavy, dark curtains, and sitting at a table at the foot of this stage is a group of women.

'Come in, come in,' a smiling, pleasant-faced woman in her late forties, and with a lot of red hair, stands up; she is eager and slightly breathless. Seated on either side of her are two other middle-aged Italian women; they too appear kindly and earnest and are dressed in the loose, vaguely ethnic clothes commonly seen on middle-class British women, but not so much on their Italian peers, who tend to favour sharper profiles, less of the dangle and drape. These are the teachers and co-ordinators of the Foreign Mothers' Group.

Also seated at the table are five very young Senegalese women, all of them slender and beautifully, vividly black, and they are laughing and talking with energy and expansive movements of their long hands. At the end of the table are two girls from Bangladesh. They are small and round and quiet. One wears a sparkly scarf, wrapped around her head. She has fat fingers and a little plump boy on her lap, who lays his cheek against hers. Last of all, there is a wiry Filipina woman, cradling a toddler who is drinking brown-coloured liquid from a bottle.

I am at least twenty-five years older than any of these girls and my circumstances could not be more different. I have infinitely more in common with the middle-aged, middle-class, white Italian school teachers than with the twenty-two-year-old Senegalese mother of three who arrived in Europe for the first time six months ago. For all that, even with my serviceable Italian, even waving the flag of an Italian spouse, even with education and experience and age, there are often, in those first months in Venice, times when I have no idea of what is going on, or what I am required to do. I have bumbled my way around post offices, school secretaries, parents' meetings, homework schedules, telephone calls to landlord, plumbers, electricians, and though for the most part I can see it for the comedy it is (for me, after all, this is play – I never have to enter the shadow of the immigration office), I am permanently two steps behind the action and, sometimes, on another planet altogether.

In Venice, where the dialect is still alive and well, people often move back and forth between Italian and Venetian. In parent and teacher meetings at the school, the discussion might well be carried out with one person speaking Italian, while the other speaks in dialect. At one such meeting, the news that there is to be a teachers' strike the following week is communicated in dialect, which is why, on the day of the strike, my children and I are the only people standing outside the locked school door. And if I knew nobody and spoke neither Italian nor Venetian, how would I be able to find out what is going on – what could I do? Would I wait there for an hour in the cold? Would I, having no idea of the working of any schools, let alone Italian ones, assume the school has closed permanently and then not go back until summoned by the social services?

There are moments when I feel confused, embarrassed, plain stupid – when everyone except me seems to understand perfectly what is going on. Looking at these young women, I think how it would be to feel really alien; multiplying to the power of a hundred my fleeting awkwardnesses and insecurities, I try to imagine being adrift in a sea of signs you cannot read, finding yourself surrounded by strangers, with strange faces, mowing sounds or gestures you cannot begin to decode, because this is a culture of which you have no knowledge whatsoever. I wonder too how it feels on the skin, to these Bangladeshi girls from their hot, crowded towns or dusty villages, who find themselves in this damp, grey, stony, silent, bewintered city in the sea, wrapped up in autumn mists, the pale faces of the people hurrying past them on the street, private and closed.

'And how do you like living in Venice?' one of the teachers asks the plump girl in the sparkly wrap, '– how is it? – good?'

The woman is all pointy eagerness as she leans across the table, urging the girl on with her straining smile. But the girl, who arrived in Italy only a few months ago, does not understand, and her cousin, sitting beside her, dressed in Western clothes, translates the question. The teacher waits, smiling, smiling. The girl nods seriously. 'Si'.

'Ah …' The teacher exhales, satisfied and sentimental, as she relaxes back into her seat, content with the answer she so badly needed.

Now she turns her attention to the cousin. 'And tell me, Amina,' she says, 'where do you live in Pakistan – oh!!' she claps her hand to her mouth, looking at her colleague, wide-eyed, mortified, 'my first gaffe! I mean –' she turns back to Amina, pink and breathless, 'I mean – Bangladesh!'

The Filipina woman produces a tub of noodles and as we eat them off plastic plates, the red-haired teacher moves around the table, photographing everyone, assiduously recording Senegalese and Bangladeshi women eating Filipino noodles. I remember all those occasions I have attended over the years, both as a teacher and as a parent – community events, family days, workshops – when other well-meaning people clicked away and filled albums or pin-up boards with photographs that were always happy mixes of black and white; old and young; male and female. And, I wonder, are the notice boards in the Houses of Parliament covered with friendly photomontages of grey-suited ministers meeting, talking, 'brainstorming'? Are the coffee tables of Downing Street scattered with albums of merry get-togethers?

The people who consider themselves to be running the serious side of life tend to meet in rooms without photographers; do not, on the whole, feel it necessary to shore themselves up with snapshots of the evidence – might, indeed, prefer to hide it.

All the same, despite my cynicism, the sweet Filipino noodles taste good and, in one of those convoluted, surreal tricks of association that history will deal out, make me too a little homesick for the familiar-unfamiliar flavours that centuries of Imperialism have made British.

The door opens again and someone else enters the room. A man, in his early fifties; baggy, well-pressed jeans hang off narrow hips and a strand of black hair has been smoothed carefully across his white scalp. He wears a spanking new tee-shirt and carries a briefcase. He approaches us beaming in the same, slightly fixed way as the red-haired woman, who rises quickly to her feet, minutely inclining towards him in the beginning of a bow.

'Can I introduce you all to the headmaster?' Her hands are clasped at chest level.

'Please, please,' the headmaster nods, smiling: we must all stand at ease. 'I didn't want to disturb you; I just wanted to say hello.'

And, wreathed in smiles, he retreats, in his immaculate leisure wear, and content, it seems, to have made an appearance.

Once the noodles have been despatched, it is time for the main business of the afternoon: the Senegalese contingent is to show us their national costume. They go to the back of the hall and, in shafts of dust-floating light cast from a high window, start taking from their bags folded pieces of bright, patterned cloth. They slip off their high-heeled shoes and begin, deftly, to wind these lengths of fabric around their hips, soon immersing their jeans in rainbow swathes. Then they take scarves and knot them around their heads, so that the stiff organza-like fabric makes turbans, or extravagant wimples – brilliant head dresses that draw these tall young women taller still: a smiling, chattering band of Amazons in this dim place. Their pleasure in themselves and their clothes fills the room like the sun.

When they have finished, they preen and parade a little, humorously, self-consciously, for us, the seated white women, old enough to be their mothers, looking on.

'Will you show us one of your dances? Please!' says the red-haired teacher.

'Oh yes,' her colleague urges them, 'please dance!'

Good-humoured, obliging, barefoot, the Senegalese girls lift up their big skirts in both hands and slap jauntily up on to the stage. A tape is pushed into a cassette player and the volume is turned up full, so that the big, bold, blaring sound of Youssou N'Dour blasts into the dank Adriatic afternoon. Then, the dance begins.

If the Italian women are hoping for some traditional display, they are disappointed. These colourful natives do not oblige with a dramatized story or ritual sequence. It is clear from the start that they are making it up as they go along.

The African girls begin to sway, vaguely at first, to the trumpet call of their man Youssou. They seem unsure which way to go. But then, suddenly, they know. Elbows go spiky-perpendicular to hips, skirts are hoiked up to reveal bent, splayed knees and they cluck and rollick and splutter in a wild, raunchy, chicken-staggering walk. They lift their tops to reveal their navels, pelvis thrust forward, muscles rolling in impromptu belly-dances. They strut and wink and shake their stuff; they prance and stagger, self-satirizing, laughing uproariously in their gorgeous, ungainly, unbridled display of comic sexuality. It is a dance to draw men and they are a scrumptious coven of colour and flesh, of loose hips, of elbows akimbo, breasts high, headgear fabulously aloft, and everything ablaze for this row of ageing European women or, is it, in defiance of them?

The red-haired teacher titters and glances sideways at her colleagues, somewhere between delight and unease. They exchange looks of self-satisfaction (the enablers, the co-ordinators), amusement and uncertainty because, there is no doubting it, in these ten minutes of misrule, five Senegalese girls have the last laugh – Big Time.

Steps

AT HALF-PAST TEN every morning, the street door bell rings. If I am at home and get to the door phone in time to ask, in the clipped, wary tone I have learnt from the Venetians: 'Chi e?', the postman's disembodied and despairing voice comes back: 'La posta', dragging out all his vowels like a Venetian Eeyore who knows that everything will go to the bad, if it hasn't already.

Occasionally I see him in the street; he is an earnest-looking, middle-aged man with thick, black-framed glasses; he has a bookish, weary look and is visibly ill-at-ease in his fluorescent yellow *Poste Italia* tabard.

If I am not at home to sign for a recorded delivery, he leaves a card on the bench in the hall. Providing a place for the dumping of such odds and ends is the only purpose now served by the two elegantly carved marble seats that flank the wide entrance. Sometimes the boys upstairs leave their Ninja Turtle backpacks on them; or a sheaf of advertisements for the Panorama Megastore in Mestre might end up there.

What purpose these benches have ever served, even in their eight-eenth-century heyday, is not obvious. They certainly imply grandeur; they suggest a charming young girl in a Longhi painting resting for a moment to catch her breath or adjusting the satin bow on her shoe, before she sallies forth into the street. The truth is, I suppose, they were never more than ornamental; probably, school bags and shopping have always been dumped on them.

Having found the *Poste Italia* card, I must now go and retrieve my package. Only a few metres off the tacky tourist jangle of the Rialto bridge, an unobtrusive entrance, on a narrow *calle*, leads into the vast, grey stone courtyard of the Central Post Office. Three tiers of open galleries run around the quadrangle and in the centre there is a marble well. The covered courtyard is cast in a permanent, monochrome stillness. The only clue that you have entered anything other than the palace of Jadis, Queen of Narnia, frozen in time, are the twisted red cord ropes, looped between brass stands, suggesting an official occasion for which crowds might imminently have to be lined up and organized.

Parcels must be fetched from an office in a far corner of the court-yard. Someone has rigged up a brown curtain across most of the window. It is the kind of curtain you might find in a heap at a jumble sale, smelling of mould. Through the window I see many wooden pigeon holes filled with packages and I watch as a tall, bearded, slightly bent man in a cardigan rifles through them hopelessly. As usual, there are several other people in the office; as usual, serving the public seems to be the least of their worries and they sit back on their chairs and chat among themselves.

After a long time, the bearded man finds my parcel. Now, I must head to another department in order to pay a bill. Making for the second floor, I walk up a great, empty stone staircase. It is unlit and unadorned. Again, there is no sign that I am either in a post office or, indeed, in the twenty-first century. The staircase is stripped of any detail of its past, and all that remains is the massive, sixteenth-century armature of the building.

Once at the top of the stairs, I push open a swing door, more suggestive of 1955 than 1555, and enter a space that is, at last, reassuringly like the kind of post offices I know. Here, there are the Formica counters and the capable, severe-looking women perched behind glass and processing the endless forms and receipts that make up so much of the substance of official Italian life. In another serpentine corral of cords and posts, the people wait, silent and passive in the inevitable queue. Every so often, it nudges wearily forward.

Because the spaces of Venice – both public and domestic – have been recycled so many times, over so many centuries, they are generally, in some way or another, ill-fitted to their current purpose. Public spaces are often very grand, but because they now house more compact enterprises and are run by many fewer people than were once needed, they seem echoey and empty. On the other hand, private apartments can be warren-like and cramped, even in the finest buildings.

But the fact is, for all its unlikely appearance, the Fondaco dei Tedeschi makes, in some ways, a fitting enough home for the Central Post Office. Built as a warehouse, market place and accommodation for the Slav and Germanic merchants trading in Venice in the sixteenth century, it still has a thoroughly practical purpose – processing the flux of letters and consignments in and out of the city.

In the early morning, the post boats are tied up outside and bundles of letters are handed down to the postmen who then distribute them around the *sestieri* or boroughs (literally: the sixths) of Venice. And in this office, on the second floor, people are queuing in the longest of traditions: supplicants, applicants, individuals who need something from the system and are required to wait, until officialdom is ready to issue a permit, an authorization, a rubber stamp.

Still, I think, as I go back down the staircase, my business done, it would be a mistake to assume nothing at all is different: the very pitch of the stairs on which I am walking gives the lie to that. These wide, marble steps force me to slow down, hobble me somehow, into a more ceremonious or respectful descent than a purpose-built, twenty-first-century post office building might require. No smart, quick, clickety-clackety trot down to street level here; the building imposes its own ancient rhythms, gives a clue to the kind of slow-stepping, low-voiced, confidential confabulations between foreign merchants as they came down, shoulder to negotiating shoulder.

Despite the fact that it continues to be used for practical business, the Fondaco dei Tedeschi is no longer a place where deals are brokered. It has gone down the scale of influence, become far less important, with its despairing, cardiganed clerks and wish-you-were-here postcards taking the place of trafficking, bartering, strutting merchants, convening in Venice from all around the globe. Its next planned incarnation as a Benetton-financed shopping centre is not, in this sense at least, news.

The uneasy relationship between the Venice in which a few thousand people live out their daily lives and the Venice that is an impossibly beautiful stage set, to which the whole gawping world flocks, is played out in the bricks and mortar of the city. Even when it is engaged in a thoroughly modern enterprise, the drag of past glories seems irresistible because, somehow, however hard it tries, Venice cannot be modern.

The controversial fourth bridge over the Grand Canal was opened in September 2008. Though its official name is the Ponte della Costituzione, it is known locally as the Calatrava Bridge, after its Spanish architect Santiago Calatrava. I know that this bridge works, both aesthetically and physically, because three times a week I walk over it with my children on our way home from judo classes at the university sports' centre. On other days, I hurry across it to the monthly farmers' market, to Freddie's tennis lesson, to visit friends in another part of the city, and this is how it works: if you are heading across the Calatrava Bridge in the direction of the railway station, you must first cross Piazzale Roma, the dowdy bus station and drop-off point quite incongruent with its role of welcoming millions of people into the world's most beautiful city. For this reason alone, Piazzale Roma inspires in me a kind of fondness: there is something comforting in its normality, its ugliness. There is also the smallest fillip of excitement to be had there, among the purring buses and car fumes, at the thought of all those places at the end of the causeway, and the roads that lead to them.

Moving towards the bridge, I dodge through the coaches, the taxis, the school kids, the men and women with their bags and brief-cases waiting to travel back into the real world on the other side of the Lagoon, and I feel as though I am in a play grown-up world. Even stepping off the road and up on to the pavement has a certain novelty, since this particular move is not possible anywhere else in this city where the only ascent and descent is either up and down stairs or off the *fondamenta* into a boat.

Then, rising from the edge of this higgledy-piggledy municipal parking lot-cum-bus station, I can see the marble foot of the new bridge. There is something in the way the wide, shallow glass steps curve upwards in a long sweep that invites you to quicken your step and widen your stride; it makes you feel suddenly lifted and for a few lovely moments drawn up into the sky. It is these moments that make of the bridge a masterpiece.

But it is not the beauty of the bridge that places this recent con-struction firmly in the ranks of Venice's glorious, secondhand spaces. There are other, far more practical considerations. Almost immediately after it is opened, people start hurting themselves on the bridge. When they aren't feeling gloriously uplifted, they are twisting their ankles and crashing to their knees. There is something in the way the stripes of metal, glass and concrete play with the eye that leads people to mis-judge their next step and fall. Add to that the fact that the many steps, elegantly pleated as a piece of Fortuny silk, are negotiable only by the entirely able-bodied and even they are in a certain amount of difficulty if they are also lugging heavy bags or pushing a child in a buggy. My shopping trolley, stuffed full of judo kit, clacks jarringly down the steps to the other side.

So, it seems, even when they come to build a major new piece of Venice at the beginning of the twenty-first century, the imperative of beauty and *bella figura* triumphs over functionality. The living city has fallen victim to its own myth.

This would certainly not have been the case when the Fondaco dei Tedeschi was built in its current form in 1508. With its 200 rooms, it would have provided a comprehensive hotel, conference centre and warehouse. It was highly functional in its conception and also impressive enough to boost the clout of those who operated there.

The fact that the Calatrava bridge is, for all its splendour, often impractical, not to say dangerous, is a subtle and depressing symbol of the demise of Venice as a place where people can really live and function efficiently from day to day. No concession has been made to the elderly, the disabled, the baby pushers, the luggage-laden, and Venice the stage set has triumphed, yet again, over Venice the city of Venetians.

Letizia and the Professor

IT IS THE last period on Friday and the top class of the Canova Middle School, Venice, is bored and restless. Their scourge and mentor, Professore Gasparini, is away at a meeting and so the mildly notorious 3E is being babysat by another teacher.

Professore Marcellio is also bored, but more by fatigue than restlessness. He is to retire at the end of the year and sits at the front of the class, slightly slumped in his crumpled cotton jacket, and shuffling vacantly through papers. The riot of sound in front of him that is twenty unfocused thirteen-year-olds might have been distant gunfire, across the border: Marcellio is elsewhere. Until, that is, he is struck in the side of the head by a missile.

The ball of paper falls into his lap and his head jerks up in time to see Francesco's cupped hand drop. The Professore fills up with a huge, weary fury, like a slowly expanding hot air balloon. He heaves to his feet, plants both meaty hands on the desk, and bellows blearily into the room:

'YOU ENGLISH!'

This is not what anyone might have expected. Francesco is indeed half English, but it is difficult to see any link between this and the paper ball that has now dropped to the floor and is lying beneath the teacher's desk.

Marcellio pulls his sagging shoulders up once more, leans harder forward, his eyes narrow with anger, and prepares to roar again:

'You ENGLISH!' His moustache flutters out this time, with the force of his rage. 'I've had enough of the LOT of you!'

Francesco's friend, my own half-English son Michael, glances nervously around. His Italian is not yet fluent, but it is clear that Marcellio's net is widening and that anybody even slightly foreign might need to look out.

'Why don't you English just get out of here, the whole damn lot of you! Clear off back to where you came from and leave us in peace!'

The silence is tight and expectant, as Marcellio draws in another gusty breath in preparation for the next blast. But before he can get it out, Letizia, who is sitting in the front row rises quickly to her feet. She too lays both hands on the table in front of her. She looks Marcellio in the eye.

'Professore,' she begins, her voice high and light. 'I would like to draw your attention to Article three of the Italian Constitution in which it states that: "All citizens have equal social dignity and are equal before the law, without distinction of gender, race, language or religion, political opinions or personal and social circumstances." '

Everyone is listening now: lanky, restless adolescent bodies suddenly still. This is good sport; this is the best.

Marcellio stares at the girl. The girl, with her elfin face and sharp black eyes, stares back. The big man's facial muscles flicker with the effort to martial thoughts, to navigate his temper; his fat hands, on the desk, flex. Then, somewhere, he finds the single impetus he needs; he opens his mouth and yells:

'I AM NOT ITALIAN! I – am – VENETIAN.'

Letizia does not miss a beat.

'Professore,' she says, 'may I draw your attention to the fact that Venice has not been an independent republic since 1797.'

PART 4: November

High Water 1

THE VERY OLD or the over-imaginative might feel unsettled by the siren. It sounds like the long, rising whine of an air raid warning as it curls plaintively up over the city in the months between October and March, alerting us to an imminent and excessive high tide: *acqua alta*.

When they hear the siren, Venetians know that they need to put on their wellies, so they can wade, with dry feet, to work or school; or that they must avoid certain *vaporetto* routes which won't be operational because an abnormally high water level is preventing the boats from clearing the bridges; or take the routes where temporary raised walkways, like long lines of trestle tables, allow you to get through the flooded areas more or less dry.

One wail of the siren tells us that the waters will climb to a metre above sea level. If this is followed by a burst of staccato beeps, you add on 10 centimetres. If there is then a second series of slightly higher beeps, that means another 10 – and so on up the scale. The beeps climb up four tones: the tide is going to rise to 140 centimetres above sea level. The city is in danger of serious flooding, perhaps even to the level of the legendarily damaging floods of 1968.

'Don't be silly,' I say, packing the children off to school briskly, after we have listened to the ever more urgent keening of the siren.

'You won't be hurt by a spot of water!'

Ten minutes later they are back.

'It's too high to get to the *vaporetto* stop,' they tell me triumphantly. I am having none of that.

'OK,' I say, pulling on my wellies, 'I'll come with you,' and I march off down the stairs, the children following behind.

Everything seems normal, until I turn the corner to the last short flight of steps leading to ground level. The metre-high stone lions that keep guard at the bottom of the stairs are practically submerged in water; only their eyes and some tufts of petrified mane are peeking out of the dirty swill. The entire hall of the building has been transformed into a swimming pool. Lewis Carroll's Alice might have been here, weeping her giant, salt tears, except that there are no birds or mice or lizards afloat in this hall, but rather shopping trolleys and bicycles and footballs – in fact, all the paraphernalia of daily life that the residents of the palazzo usually leave on the ground floor, to avoid hulking it upstairs to their apartments.

I slow down, but do not stop. The water is only a few centimetres below the top of my boots, so I advance carefully, wading across the wide hall. When I reach the front door, the pressure of the current out in the *calle* is so strong that I have to lean hard to force it ajar. Once outside, the scene in narrow, grey Calle del Vin is not far off apocalyptic. People are wading urgently through the rising water, but in a kind of nightmarish slow motion, with their belongings held above their heads and coats gathered up to their waists. The water through which they are pressing is neither glistening nor limpid nor blue, but an unleashed cesspit. Every bit of vile and filthy detritus imaginable swirls there – human shit, rotten food, a family of drowned baby rats. The drains of the city have disgorged their worst.

Gleefully, Freddie launches himself into this disgusting broth and within five seconds is soaked to the waist.

'OK,' I say, with the same masterful decisiveness I adopted five minutes ago, at the top of the stairs, 'back inside!'

For the next hour, we watch from the fourth floor, as normal life continues to retreat from the canal turned flood torrent below. For a while, the welly wearers struggle staunchly on, but before long the water level rises too high and this is when the men in waders begin to appear – fishermen, boatmen, the real water professionals, with the professional kit.

When the tide eventually gets too high even for waders, boats are the only solution, except that soon it stops being possible to pass under any of the bridges and the small craft begin to navigate around them, over the submerged pavements. The last people we see daring the waters, now at the maximum level of 1.4 metres, are two canoeists, jaunty in their fluorescent orange rain jackets, who double over flat as their canoe slides under the bridge, and clears it with only a few centimetres to spare.

As the day goes on, friends and relatives call us from different parts of the world to ask what's going on. They have seen the dramatic television footage of Piazza San Marco submerged in water and imagine us islanded and in a state of emergency. But of course the truth is, by the middle of the day, the waters have gone back down; *acqua alta* is not a flood, but a very high tide that can turn nasty. Which is why, the next morning, the bright early sunshine reveals a city quietly drying out. The shops and restaurateurs with premises at ground level are stoically stacking chairs and tables and unrolling sodden carpets outside in the *calle*. They spend the morning with buckets and mops, swabbing down the floors and walls of their properties. Their good humour and resignation as they get on with the job say just one thing: there's nothing to be done; this is how things are in Venice.

High Water 2

RISING WATER IS not the only threat to Venice. There are other tides that flood the city every day of the year and threaten its existence in very different ways. Each year about 16.5 million tourists pass through the city; this has a devastating effect on the resident community. Anybody who has known Venice over the past two decades is painfully aware of this and also of the frightening speed at which change is taking place.

When I met Alberto nineteen years ago, he was making violins in a workshop on a canal at the west of the city. At around half-past twelve I would call by, passing from the baking, white stones of the *fondamenta* into this cool, dim space. The walls were unclad stone; the ceiling was striped with ancient, blackened beams. It smelt rich and sweet – of linseed oil and varnish and wood – which made me think of frankincense and myrrh.

I would sit on one of Alberto's high stools while he finished off a piece of work at his bench before lunch. Once, when I arrived, he was sketching a violin scroll in pencil, on a block of wood. Then, with a fine knife, he began to carve the image into three dimensions. Over the following days, I saw the scroll emerging delicately from the wood, like a fern uncurling.

Here, in Alberto's workshop, an antique craft was being pursued, but the students from the *Conservatorio* and the musicians who came in for repairs or to buy a new instrument were, of course, as modern as anybody anywhere. This was Venice at its best: a place of artisanal excellence, keeping alive ancient traditions and techniques for the modern world.

When Alberto had finished what he was doing, he would close the dark green shutters and we would go out, locking the shop behind us.

At the bar around the corner, we often found Luigi drinking coffee and smoking his pipe in the corner. The dry, mildly piratical painter had his studio close to Alberto's workshop and they were friends.

At other times, Daniele and Pietro might be there too. Their bookshop, Patagonia, was opposite the bar. Slight, wry, bookish Pietro with his hunched shoulders and pebble spectacles, and his business partner Daniele, Venetian wideboy and self-ironizing literary showman, made an odd couple, but their shop was a fine space for browsing or chatting and a small local centre for literary events – talks, readings, discussions.

These were the four energetic, creative men I came to know when they were working on one small Venetian block, in 1982.

When I return to Venice in 2009, Alberto's workshop has become an office for a company organizing tourist lets; Patagonia has gone and a kebab shop has taken its place; and Luigi has left his studio for cheaper premises on the mainland.

This is a small anecdote, of course, but it reflects bigger and more widespread processes in a city where the tourist dollar is king and the inhabitants struggle to keep their environment alive and adapted to a rich daily life.

One morning, I have a doctor's appointment. The surgery is some distance from where I live, but I set off in good time and head for the *vaporetto* stop. The boat is moving towards the stop as I arrive, but there are so many people waiting there that I cannot get on. This would be frustrating anywhere and might happen in any city in the world; but what makes it different in Venice is, that as I stand watching the *vaporetto* glide off, I see that the boat is packed full of tourists with that dreamy, relaxed holiday look plastered all over their faces. I feel a disproportionate rage swelling in me – I cannot go about my daily business because these people have overrun the public transport system. Evidently no one individual is to blame here but, like it or not, this is how Venetians – born and adopted – often feel.

Thrusting down my bitter thoughts, I abandon the boat option and set off at a run towards the surgery. Often there are alternative, back routes to be taken in Venice, but this particular journey unavoidably involves passing along a main drag between one tourist hotspot and another.

The words 'main drag' suggest something wide and boulevardish; this main drag, however, is a very narrow alley, only just wide enough for two people to walk abreast, and it is stuffed with tourists. I am stuck behind a clot of people for a few seconds, then, seeing a gap ahead, sprint around the man in front and manage to get ahead. The illusion of speed is temporary though, because I now find myself at a total standstill behind a group that has stopped to admire the window display in a mask shop. Having wriggled my way past this impediment, I am now slowed right down by a couple who are trundling along, pulling their suitcases on wheels behind them. There are two Venetian women ahead of me and I can practically see the smoke coming out of their ears.

'Why the hell can't they just pick up the suitcases and carry them?' one of them says loudly to the other. Her tone is rude; the tourists are, in a sense, innocent – certainly unaware – but the point is this: the city is not functioning for the people who live here.

I arrive late for my appointment, very hot and sweaty and red in the face.

'I'm sorry,' I say to the doctor, 'there were so many tourists, I couldn't get on the boat. I had to walk and that was impossible too.'

The doctor is a sweet-faced elderly woman.

'*Povera Venezia* – poor Venice,' she says sadly. 'What hope is there?'

Meanwhile, out beyond the Lido and Pellestrina, the vast concrete structure of the Mose is being built in the Adriatic Sea. This system of barriers designed to control the high waters, and costing around six billion euros, is a controversial attempt to control the high waters. Scheduled to be completed in 2011, it is still being constructed. On the mainland side of the city, however, absolutely nothing is being done to stem the vast tide of tourists flowing incessantly into Venice and drowning its daily life, its heart and soul.

San Martino Went Up to the Attic

'*San Martin xè andà in sofita*
A trovar la so novizia
La so novizia non ghe gera
'L xè cascà con cul per tera
El s'à messo 'n boletin
Viva, viva San Martin.'

('St Martin went up to the attic
To find his fiancée.
His fiancée was not there,
St Martin fell flat on his bottom
And put a bandage on himself.
Hurrah, hurrah, St Martin!')

ON 11 NOVEMBER Venetians celebrate the feast day of San Martino, an early Christian saint, who met a freezing beggar on the road and, in an act of somewhat qualified largesse, cut his cloak in two, giving half to the ragged man.

For a few days before the festival the windows of the cake shops of Venice fill with biscuit cut-outs of San Martino on his horse, draped in the as-yet unsevered mantle. They are iced in bright colours and crudely decorated with hundreds and thousands, silver balls, chocolates and sweets. The biggest and showiest of them can be as much as a metre high, but they are usually the size of a cake.

The feast of San Martino belongs to the children of the city. In the late afternoon, when the winter dark has fallen, they take pots and pans and wooden spoons and troop around their neighbourhood, bashing their tinny homemade drums with gusto and going from shop to shop singing the song of San Martino and asking for goodies. The shopkeepers hand over sweets or fruit and the children come home laden with edible loot.

In the busy shopping street near to Calle del Vin, you see the little groups of kids, wrapped up tight in coats, hats and scarves, scampering between the shops in a state of high excitement, while a protective parent lingers tactfully in the shadows.

But now, a potent competitor to the time-honoured Venetian ritual has arrived in the city and its threat lies in its very similarity to the Feast of San Martino.

This festival, which is itself an ancient rite, but relatively new to Italy, takes place ten days before San Martino, on 31 October. It has many of the same ingredients: the thrill of being out on the hunt, after dark, on a wintry evening, with your hot breath pluming into the chill air; the jewel-like brightness of the shops as their lights flood out into the night, and their promise of good things; a rhyme or song declaimed in return for gifts of sweets and a general licence to shout and crash and announce your presence wherever you go, in the company of other gleeful children.

But the imported Hallowe'en has an added glamour, with which San Martino – pious as he is – simply cannot compete. The problem is an old one: the Devil and his doings are altogether more titillating and entertaining than all the goodness in the world, even if it is dressed up with the bait of sweets, and biscuits shaped like a man on horseback. What San Martino lacks is the glamour of evil, the thrill of ghostly fear.

In this period of transition and, I suspect, inevitable usurpation, of the saint's feast day by the forces of devilish (American) Misrule, the children of Venice are enjoying a brief season of double glut. On 31 October, they pour into the streets in ghoulish masks, black capes and witches' hats and descend on the shopkeepers, calling out: 'Dolcetto o scherzetto!' ('Sweet or trick!'). Then, a mere ten days later, they set out again, singing San Martino's song, hands out for another handout. Some shopkeepers refuse to give anything for Hallowe'en, telling them to come back the following week for San Martino, but the majority are indulgent of both festivals and vast quantities of sweets are consumed.

This is not simply a swallowing up of the old ways by the new. Hallowe'en is most likely a considerably more ancient jamboree than the saint's day, which might be seen as another of the beatified shop windows in which early Christianity advertised its pious credentials. Either way, they both overlap with end of harvest rituals, marking the transition from summer to winter.

Does the gradual demise of the festival of San Martino matter all that much? Perhaps not: the passing of any pleasure or happy memory has its melancholy edge, but traditions are mutating or perishing or appearing all the time and all over the world. The Venetian anxiety about the loss of San Martino has more to do with that peculiarly Venetian problem of feeling that the indigenous life of the city is so very fragile that every blow, however slight, may be terminal.

In the meantime, my friend Ginevra is altogether more pragmatic:

'Well,' she says, as we watch our kids go rampaging off in full witchy and ghostly regalia on 31 October, 'it's no surprise Hallowe'en is winning. It's just much more fun being bad.'

Trailing Clouds of Glory

> *'... trailing clouds of glory do we come*
> *From God, who is our home:*
> *Heaven lies about us in our infancy!*
> *Shades of the prison-house begin to close*
> *Upon the growing Boy ...'*

(From Wordsworth's 'Ode to Immortality')

THE PARENTS OF the children of 3E wander into the classroom. We take off our coats, prop up our dripping umbrellas and, still faintly exuding the damp of the Venetian November evening outside, we sit down in the circle of chairs laid out for us.

Several of the teachers are already seated at an L-shaped arrangement of tables placed at the front of the class. This layout suggests either that we are gathered here as an audience for a panel of experts or else that we are the shuffling-in accused, but despite the hierarchical furniture arrangements, the atmosphere is relaxed and people are chatting amiably. As is so often the case in Italy, no one appears to regard themselves as inferior to anyone else, but the conventions are being observed.

Professor Gasparini arrives – last and to a certain effect – as befits his station as teacher of Italian and unofficial head of year. He is a diminutive man, but all muscle, and he has a serious handshake. I like a strong handshake. I practise a strong handshake. But Gasparini's handshake is mythic. It is a handshake you must survive in order to continue the Quest. Whenever we meet, I spend ten minutes afterwards straightening out my crushed fingers.

Every inch of Gasparini expresses determination, direction and, above all, Opinion. He sits at the central point of the High Table, the other, female, teachers flanking him like a Prada-clad Praetorian Guard. We wait in silence.

First, Gasparini presses the fingertips of both hands together like a doctor in a 1950s film (he lacks only the crisp white coat and the stethoscope). He breathes in deeply, looks severely at us through his black-framed glasses (something of the Clark Kent here); he sighs heavily; he goes in.

'To tell you the truth: it's no good.'

And so it unfolds: our children, Gasparini regrets to have to inform us, are a bunch of bright, badly behaved ne'er-do-wells. They fail to do their homework and are simply not sufficiently respectful of their teachers.

'Yes,' chips in the maths teacher, Professoressa Zapputti, 'and do you know what they've started doing in my lessons?' She pauses theatrically; she scans her audience. 'They imitate me! They repeat everything I say! It's just no good.'

She frowns and everybody – parents and teachers – nod gravely.

It strikes me that in Britain, the day a teacher speaks publicly in this way, is Judgement Day: that terrible moment when she has finally given up. The failed pedagogue who, after years of struggle, can take no more, has cracked under the pressure and will now, wiping the tears from her eye, slink from the room and into early retirement, a broken woman.

Is this Professoressa Zapputti? Oh no. Zapputti is a short, square, ageing and glamorous blonde, with a flirtatious smile and robust upper arms. Michael quakes at the mere mention of her. Zapputti by name, I obscurely, onomatopoeically think, is ZAPPUTTI! by nature: a kind of mathematical Superwoman to Gasparini's Literary Superman. The cultural assumptions behind her words are, once again, the complete opposite of those one would find in Britain. It is a logic untarnished by guilt or by any undue sense of personal responsibility; it is utterly unclouded by the possibility that she herself might be at fault. To Zapputti and, it seems, to all the other people assembled here, the situation is clear: the children of 3E are not behaving acceptably and that is their fault. The mood is one of solidarity: nobody is blaming anybody else. These kids are forces of nature and we, their civilized elders and betters, must work together to tame them.

Now, one of the fathers speaks up.

'Professore Gasparini,' he begins pleasantly, 'I am a little confused. Clearly the children have made a mistake, but when you say that only two out of eighteen did their geography homework last week, I wonder if, perhaps, there was some kind of misunderstanding – a problem of communication. On the part of the kids, obviously.'

Yes, yes, Gasparini nods sagely, they must have failed to understand. The father sits back in his chair, apparently satisfied. The matter does not appear to me to have advanced at all. I must have missed something.

So far, so united. Then, a mother raises her hand to speak; she is small, plump and has a lot of bouncy brown hair.

'And French?' she asks emphatically.

There is a palpable change in the atmosphere: a drawing in of breath, a collective pursing of the lips. The French teacher, Professoressa Maestri, is not present, but far from this restraining anyone from discussing her, it seems to give them licence. The Professoressa has been absent so much, the plump mother goes on, that the children are learning no French at all. What is to be done about this?

While she delivers this indignant speech, the teachers nod and smile sympathetically. Then Gasparini speaks:

'Well, Signora, obviously as her colleagues, we are not in a position to discuss the situation. You would need to speak with the headmaster.'

He smiles benignly and is clearly in agreement with everything the woman has been saying. This is no closing of ranks, no serious refusal to comment on the matter. Quite the reverse. I think of poor Maestri – a pretty, hectically over-made-up woman who, it is said, is struggling with a long journey to work from the mainland, a young child and her obvious inability to teach high-spirited thirteen-year-olds. But the plump mother has not finished yet.

'And you, Signora,' she continues, turning now to a teaching assistant sitting on the outer flank of the High Table. 'From your more detached position – would you say the children are under control in the French lessons?'

The elderly, impeccably coiffed assistant smirks in this unexpected limelight.

'Quite honestly, no,' she says happily and, judging by the general nodding and smiling, it seems that everyone is satisfied with this reply.

The absent Maestri, with her wide, nervous blue eyes, her harum scarum mascara and too-red lipstick, is unaware, for now, of the knife twisting in her back, and I see that respect and professional solidarity go only so far here. The weak are shown no mercy.

Now, the meeting is ending. People are standing up and beginning to leave and one of the mothers approaches Zapputti.

'Professoressa,' I hear her say deferentially. 'I know my Giovanni was one of those behaving rudely and I would like to apologize for his behaviour.'

Zapputti accepts the apology graciously, regally even. A particular vision of the world remains intact: children are to be duly respectful to adults. We, their parents and teachers, must ensure that they conform to our rules and expectations and that they grow up acknowledging the authority of their elders and betters.

Here, in this dreary Venetian school room, with nothing on the yellowing walls except one large, lopsided map of the world; where the work is often difficult and dry and unimaginative, there is still this consensus between parents, teachers and children. The kids muck around; the teachers complain; the parents rant and apologize. It is a ramshackle business, as human relations and human solutions generally are, but everyone is playing the same game by the same rules. In that sense, at least, it works.

Salute!

THE PEOPLE THRONGING good-naturedly through the streets are almost all locals. Any tourists are incidental to this most Venetian of holidays and, just for a change, barely intrude. A pontoon bridge has been set up across the Grand Canal and thousands of people are moving slowly over it, all day long, passing from San Marco to Dorsoduro in the annual pilgrimage to the Basilica of Santa Maria della Salute, where they will give thanks to God for the end of the plague that devastated the city in 1630.

In good Venetian style, the shocked gratitude of the survivors was expressed architecturally, in the construction of Longhena's church with its great snail coils of masonry and ballooning domes. This is our destination on a chill, grey November afternoon nearly 400 years later.

As I shuffle forward with the crowd, I look over the edge of the bridge and see below a slight, white egret, with brilliant green feet, standing on one of the bridge's supports. The bird is utterly still; the crowd clatters overhead. We come off the votive bridge and pack into a narrow *calle*. Moving on, under an archway, there is a dense press of bodies and the air is cold, damp and steaming. Even in this dark tunnel between buildings, the tall man next to me goes on smoking. We emerge into the paved space in front of the church that widens out before us like a river delta into which the streams of people are pouring. This area gives on to the Grand Canal and is lined with stalls selling candles to the pilgrims. The candles are heaped up extravagantly – some are a metre high and two handspans round. I buy four of a more modest size with patchy little transfers of the Madonna stuck on the wax, one for each of my children. Against the odds and a certain amount of vociferous public opinion, Freddie and Roland try to fence with their candles as we carry on, at the crowd's shuffling pace, up the broad steps of the church.

Inside, the Basilica is like a vast, fat bud opening from its circular centre into the petals of chapels. To the right as we enter, the crowd is gathered ten deep around an iron grid on legs. It is the size and shape of a large table and dozens of candles have been wedged into the many holes; they make gross stalagmites of dripping wax and spindly, dwindling outcrops. The whole glowing white mass veers to one side and seems to be on the brink of collapse. Two girls in efficient brown overalls and heavy duty gloves are quickly removing half-burnt candles, snuffing them out and piling them on one side. Then, they take the fresh candles held out to them by the people pressing up to the barrier, light them, and stick them into whatever space they can find in the crude candelabra.

The Festival of the Salute is part of real life in this city, an integral element in the cycle of every year. Unlike the hollow and showy

Carnival – reinvented for the tourists and universally detested by Venetians – this is not an exotic spectacle. Well-polished and pragmatic locals in their uniformly dull-coloured padded jackets, sensible shoes, hats, gloves and scarves have a plain, provincial look which is almost comically counter-balanced by their lavish Basilica with its stone angels and saints, its extravagant spirals and domes. There is a dogged normality in the way these people gossip in clusters, while the great space of the church around them fills with perfumed drifts of incense, and at the High Altar the priestly celebrants follow their ritual course, beneath the gaze of the Black Madonna, the gold-encrusted, twelfth-century Byzantine icon turned, somehow, wallpaper.

As we edge forward to hand over our candles, I see how this ritual has, in certain ways, barely changed over centuries. Here are the same keen-faced, beady-eyed, wiry-framed Venetians; the handsomely cassocked priests and their antique chants; the whine and thud of dialect. But then, of course, it is also dramatically different: no more rankly stinking bodies or breath; strong white teeth, smooth hands and bright blond hair are everywhere. The vigorous and smart fifty- and sixty-year-olds milling around here would once have been the aged, the toothless and the bent. Now, nobody is hump-backed, no one limps or lisps as a result of polio, bad hips or cleft lips. And the dialect spoken is mostly diluted by the pretty melodies of modern Italian to mere accent, proverb and fragments of the original Venetian.

But despite these obvious differences, this short, local pilgrimage of thanks is not an empty re-enactment of a long dead history, wiped in all but name from the communal memory. Nearly four hundred years ago, in these Venetian streets, these houses, these squares, every second person you knew was dead or horribly dying. The person next to you. Your intimate, busy, handsome, prosperous city had been transformed, overnight, into a hell hole, a charnel house, a place where malign and unstoppable forces were battling for the souls of your children, your friends – for your very own soul.

On the elegant marble benches in the hall of our building, where we rest our shopping bags or stop to pick up a parcel left there by the postman, the pall bearer of 1630 had slumped for a few minutes' rest before grunting to his companions that they must once again shoulder up the sorry corpse they had somehow managed to manouevre down the stairs and take it on its way to disposal. Stinking, buboed bodies had piled up in the *calle* where I now drop a carrier bag of rubbish in the mornings, in time for the arrival of the 8.30 a.m. refuse boat.

In those terrible days of 1630, the skin of your warm child sup-purated in front of your eyes, rotting before she was even dead. Pain and disfigurement, decay and loss were smeared on the walls of these narrow streets, as though some monstrous and vengeful hand had dropped a titan's boulder in the stillness of the Lagoon and a tidal wave of devastation had ringed out from it.

And, of course, over years, over generations, the circles widened and thinned until the memory of all that horror was no longer concrete, but became the echo of memories. What was, in 1630, an unbearable grief had transformed, by 1655, to buried sadness; by 1700 it had worn down to bitterness, which modified, slowly, across the ensuing decades, into a certain grumpiness of character. This in turn transmuted over sub-sequent generations into a marked stubbornness which was the merest shadow of the resignation arising from past grief. This, in a great, great, great grandson of a plague survivor, had become a certain dourness of look or abruptness of manner. All of these might be qualities, reactions, behaviours that had their roots in that original, terrible cataclysm.

How much of what any of us are has drifted down in this way from the past, like sticks caught up in black-matted flotsam, then dislodged again, back into the current? Running down the stairs from their apartments, to get to school or work, the inhabitants of Venice do not think of the stumbling, sweating seventeenth-century pall bearers, hulking a sad cargo down these same steps, between these same walls. But the city is still their place, as it was their ancestors', and in celebra-tion of that, as much as anything else, they continue to file up the steps of the Salute, with candles in their hands.

Here on this dank November afternoon I am witness to a crum-pling up of time. By walking in the footsteps of their forebears, by joining the flow with them and continuing to give thanks for delivery from something that terribly mattered, the Venetians are keeping in their lives ampler realities than that of the lone individual wading through the short, muddied span of one life.

Virginia Woolf describes how, when reading Chaucer, 'we are floated up to him insensibly on the current of our ancestors' lives'. Moving through the ancient streets of Venice, adapting their contemporary life to the spaces and rituals of past generations, modern Venetians are floated up to their ancestors on the currents of art, habit and endeavour.

In the Salute, named for health and ill health, the lottery of mortality and the hope of eternal redemption are enshrined in a divinely inspiring space. Standing among ordinary Venetians, in an extraordinary building, on an ordinary winter's day, giving ritual thanks for a temporary deliverance from sickness and death is, perhaps, as close to stepping out of linear time as I will ever get.

Only by participating in the past – its griefs and rhythms – by looking death and suffering in the face and every so often acknowledging it as ours, do we have a hope in hell of survival. Do we have a hope of remembering that, in other parts of our planet, now, in this minute, whole cities are in the stranglehold of illness, of hunger; are being besieged by crazed armies; are living a present that is, thank God, for now, our past and holiday memory.

PART 5: December

Undercover Tourist

SNOW AND HIGH water come together on the same Saturday in December – one dropping silently from the sky, the other gurgling up from the drains. I have a parcel to fetch from the post office at the Rialto, and at 9 o'clock I set off. The Accademia bridge is deserted as I drag my trolley behind me, up the snow-muffled steps. A bitter wind blows along the Grand Canal from the Adriatic.

Once on the other side of the bridge, I meet an American friend, steadfastly crunching across Campo Santo Stefano in wellies and a sheepskin hat with ear flaps, determined to open her gallery on time. A little further on, I come to one of the lowest points of the city and find the *calle* flooded with rank-smelling, icy water surging around my ankles. I gather the skirts of my overcoat in both hands and wade, very gingerly, on.

After the bitter, monochrome of the streets, the sorting office spills yellow light and warmth out of the door. It is full of postmen in sweaters and a holiday mood, who have been reprieved from their long morning trudge from door to door by the extreme weather conditions. These are just about the only Venetians I encounter during the whole morning. Who, after all, in their right mind, would set foot outside the house in such weather? The entire round trip (an easy forty-minute walk, under normal conditions) takes me two hours of wading, half slipping and half freezing.

At the *vaporetto* stop, temporary walkways have been laid out for the high water. Some Japanese tourists are edging along them, looking for the right boat stop, and for all the world as if they might be blown away at any moment by the vicious north wind. They are giggling nervously and, being seriously under-dressed, are blue in the face. I can only think that they are utterly perplexed: what kind of a way is this to conduct one's life, in a wealthy country, in the twenty-first century?

At the boat stop, I hear someone calling my name. It is Katerina and her niece, two stalwart Moldovan cleaners for whom I suppose this is a picnic in comparison with their own eastern winter. They are pink-cheeked and good-humoured; their black hair is obscured by brightly printed shawls, and each looks as though she might have stepped out of another, larger version of herself, in a stack of Russian dolls.

Almost everyone I meet on the street today is a foreigner. Whether visitor or immigrant, we would reveal our true alien colours to any Venetian through the mere fact of being out at all. It is at times like this that I know with conviction that my fragile sense of belonging here is an illusion to which I cling, but which cannot outlast my time in the city. Despite not having lived in London for sixteen years, I can still be a Londoner. When I step out of Paddington Station, I am part of the real life in those streets and even if I don't know exactly how to buy a ticket for the bus any more, I am still at home, albeit a dithery old-timer. In Venice – a village under siege from foreigners – you can win temporary acceptance by living daily life here, but when you leave, you are, once again, forever a tourist.

Which is why, even as a resident, I face the reality and the risk of being an alien every single time I leave my house. On a good day, I do not have to think about it. On a good day, I scuttle along my little rat run of friendly faces: the parents at the school gate and the teachers; the sweet-faced woman from Sant'Erasmo on the market stall; the loquacious cake shop owner with her wonderful pastries; the helpful man in the health store; the kindly, melancholy ice cream lady; the laddishly jolly tennis coach, the music teachers, the neighbours and friends – and I feel happy, welcomed and accepted. But on other days, if I should happen to diverge from this circuit of known faces who, far more importantly, know *me*, I might well be stung – both financially and socially – by any number of hostile locals.

If I go into the wrong bar and ask, in my foreign accent, for a coffee, I may automatically pay twice what the man next to me is paying with his singsong of a Venetian accent. Not only do I pay twice the money, but I pay also for being a stranger, with the off-hand, unsmiling manner of the waitress, the palpable contempt of the shopkeeper. I find myself, pathetically, wanting to plead with them, waving my credentials in their faces:

'But my kids are at school here, you know! I live just down the street, all year round! Treat me kindly – please ... Allow me to belong ...'

Although there is never an excuse for rudeness, here, in this beleaguered little community, there are numerous reasons for it. So I have to admit that if these people continue to look at me with disdain, they are, from a certain point of view, justified in doing so. After all, what am I in this city other than an undercover tourist? A parasitic sucker of the Venetian blood; playing, in their home, at belonging?

But you could, of course, turn all of that around. Venice, though now a village, was, and should be again, a city. Cities are ample places – where change is the continuum; where new blood breeds new life. And all sorts of different foreigners come to cities: the welcome and unwelcome, the temporary, the permanent. The trouble is that when, as here, a siege is on, nothing really comes in or goes out.

I never wanted to be an undercover tourist. Quite the opposite, but I cannot fully belong here because Venice does not allow it. The city closes itself up, turns its back on the world which, with careless sentimentality, ruthlessly exploits its charms. Like the victim of violence, Venice can no longer distinguish between those who will cherish and commit to it, and those who want only to exploit.

'Do you *know*?' I hear an American guide drawl at an incredulous tourist group, waving her hand magisterially along the length of the Giudecca. 'Those aren't hotels over there. They are *real* houses where *real* people live! And they have shops which only *six* people can get into at a time!'

It's time for the cut-price airlines, the cruise ships, the hotel chains, the tour operators to lay off the relentless onslaught. To leave this damaged city in peace for a while so that it can rebuild confidence, relearn to appreciate diversity and change, safe from the brutal mono-flux of tourism. Where is the political vision that will encourage small businesses and artisans to return to the ancient workshops? That will provide affordable housing in Venice, for the people who are born, live and die here? Where are the politicians who see that the human race cannot go on in this way – consuming everything in sight – and that this unique city offers a visionary blueprint for small-scale living, close community, sustainability?

'No, Venice is finished,' says Gianfranco. He is the committed director of a municipal project of rare imagination and creativity – a rush of optimistic fresh air into the community. 'Ten years ago, my building was full of residents. Now, my family is the only one living here and all the other apartments are holiday flats. When we come out on to the landing, there are different people there every day. Usually, they don't even say good morning.'

'I lived in San Stae until six years ago,' Monica tells me. 'My family had been there for generations, but then the landlord realized that the short-term tourist lets were going to make him much, much more money, so he chucked us out.'

'No,' says the friendly woman I am chatting to on the *vaporetto*, as we head out for the beach at the Lido, on a Saturday morning, with our children. "We don't live here any more. Since we had our children, we can't afford to stay. We've got a house in Mestre now. But you know, I never stop wanting to come home.'

We can all imagine a Venice submerged by the waters of the Lagoon. This may yet happen, but what about fostering in the meantime a shorter-term vision of the city's future, which, linked as it is to the sustainable and the local, might offer a model of change, not apocalypse.

In this picture of the future, the houses that have been packed with short-let holiday flats fill up again with families and people who live their real, daily lives here. The shiny, skin-deep tourist outlets flogging masks and scarves are reclaimed by butchers and bakers and grocers who sell the stuff of life – meat, bread and milk. In this Venice of the future, the deserted streets and courtyards come alive again, bubbling with a new generation of kids who, on hot days, dive-bomb from bridges into the water.

Growing Up in History

AT A PARTY, I meet a Venetian woman who is about to leave the city and go with her young children to live on *terraferma*. She is rather elegant, with melancholy eyes.

'What makes me sad,' she tells me, 'is that they will not grow up in all this beauty.'

I have often noticed how much Venetians speak of the loveliness of their city. I suppose that the changing dimensions of the place – always charming, sometimes just plain wondrous – never stop being surprising, even after a lifetime.

So much of Venice is on a small scale: the narrow byways and cramped apartments giving a feeling of containment, of the local and familiar. Then, every so often, as one moves around the city, this intimacy undergoes a dramatic transformation. It is as though you are paddling happily in a shallow stream, take one step more, and find yourself on the brink of a vast and vertiginously plunging waterfall: all spume and glitter and cascading, silken perspective. The fishing village turned Shangri-La.

In the depths of our first winter, I take Freddie to see a doctor near Campo Santa Maria Formosa. We are unfamiliar with this part of the city and are trying to find our way through a maze of anonymous, dank-smelling *calli* with dark, water-streaked walls. The sky overhead is a flat, black strip.

As with all routes navigated for the first time and at night, it feels long and tortuous. I hesitate at every junction or bridge, not sure whether I have completely lost my way. Freddie trots along beside me, holding my hand. Then, with no warning at all, instead of leaving one

97

tight little *calle* and entering another, we find ourselves on the edge of space. A trick of the darkness, of street lights or perspective, shows a wide expanse of pale stone pavement sloping upwards to touch the walls of the Church of Santa Maria Formosa. No water, no grass, nobody: a stone edifice rising from a sea of stone, looming white, arctic, against the night sky. The small boy at my side lets out a sharp breath: 'Ah!' No words for this mysterious, sudden vision that has, in that instant, so radically altered his six-year-old's perceptions, turning the physical world into something grand and ghostly.

What does it feel like to live in this place if you are a child and still adrift in those years when what is inside your head and what is outside are often indistinguishable? My children hang from the back of the boat as it scuds through the choppy waters of the north Lagoon to the Lido. They lay their cheeks on the cold metal bar and shout into the eruptions of froth and the wind. They watch the Christmas decorations going up along the rio and see the strings of white lights reflected in the still, chill, black water. They hopscotch down the dirty *calle* when there has been no rain for days and then, all of a sudden, there is *acqua alta* and they are knee deep in salt water. When school is cut off by this high water, they make Lego boats and play with them in the street turned river. Their world has dissolved in the space of an hour, into something unimaginably different – a waterborne playground.

When my eldest son Michael moves to the senior school in Venice, he enters the hushed halls of a seventeenth-century palace. The atmosphere is monastic: grey, calm, unadorned. It is a strangely empty place. Despite the size of the building, one teacher explains to me, the numbers of pupils are strictly limited by health and safety regulations. This, it occurs to me, is the unlikely spectacle of twenty-first-century bureaucracy coming to the rescue of the monkish, the collegiate and the classical.

Michael's lessons take place in high-ceilinged rooms that would once have been the richly furnished and decorated apartments of an aristocratic Venetian household. Over the door frame in his classroom there is a stucco oval relief. It is held up, like a large egg, by two crumple-bottomed cherubim; at its centre a Grecian hero, in his pony-tail helmet, sits ruminatively – more, it must be said, of a foppish eighteenth-century youth than a hellenic superman.

The rooms are bare except for some plastic-topped tables and metal-legged, stackable chairs, circa 1972, which are lined up in front of a blackboard scrawled all over with columns of Latin verbs. The only other contemporary addition, besides the single electric light bulb hanging down on a very long cord from the very high ceiling, is a map of Greece. Whether the cultural reference points implicit in this map, or these teetering piles of verbs or indeed the blackboard upon which they are written can actually be described as contemporary is debatable; let's just say that they arrived in the room more recently.

In this environment, adolescent Italians are swallowing industrial quantities of Latin and Greek every day. This is the Liceo Classico – the most academic of the state-financed senior schools – in which the curriculum is still strikingly similar to that of the ancient Greeks from whom it takes its name: philosophy, literature, languages, mathematics. The only subject that has all but lapsed since classical times is athletics, which may explain the dejected and slightly flabby appearance of the Grecian youth over the door and also the trapped and dazed look one often sees on the faces of the latter-day students.

Here at the Classico the approach to learning is dry and mercilessly rigorous. Within months of his arrival, my son is tackling serious bits of Homer. Because he is struggling with his Greek I go to talk with his teacher. I mention, in the course of our discussion, how much he loves reading the Greek myths.

'Ah, but you see,' she explains gently and a little patronizingly, 'the Classico isn't about *enjoying* the myths. Michael's work here is to learn the grammar of ancient languages.'

So, in these still, elegant and understated spaces 300 teenagers sit for hours on end, tackling big concepts and boring, repetitive tasks. There must be days when they are overwhelmed with inertia in this environment which could not be more different from the small-scale, two-dimensional, constantly moving virtual world of the internet in which they are also growing up – both imaginatively and conceptually.

The speed and colour and noise of the modern media must seem to them so terribly absent in these echoing, monochrome halls. When Michael gets home from school and flops down in front of the computer, his relief is practically audible. School can be horribly tedious at times and also very, very difficult. Little account is taken of individual expression or spontaneous creativity in the study programmes; you either like it, lump it, or get out.

At the same time, I can see that the young people who survive these places (and many don't last the course, peeling off to other, less heroic but more forgiving institutions) are astonishingly knowledgeable: they have great swathes of *The Odyssey* by heart, they can quote you Dante and translate Ovid without batting an eyelid. They are the last remaining standard bearers of a 2,500-year-old culture and there is, for me, both value and a kind of crazy nobility in that.

And then there's the question of boredom. I hang on to the conviction that we need the grey spaces in our days; that without the pauses, the daydreaming, the absences, the silence, there is nowhere for imagination and meditative thought to take root. If life is constantly played out on the same sensory plane, centimetres from a screen, if there are no changes of perspective, no refiguring of dimensions outside of a virtual arena, how can we ever be surprised into new or different ways of perceiving?

But how can I communicate to my son, who was born in 1998, that this extraordinary, archaic system, still and only just lumbering on like a dinosaur across Italy, might be of interest or in any way valuable to him? Of course, when parents say just about anything to their adolescent children, it is, by definition, like word coming through from the Jurassic. This has always been the case, but it is clear to me, all the same, that at this particular point in history the gap between the generations is especially yawning.

When I first went to university in 1981, I stood, like a medieval clerk, at high wooden desks in the library and thumbed through dog-eared cards in a long wooden drawer, with copper half-moon handles, that were marked Ab – Acc, in order to track down the book I needed.

In 1985, when I returned to postgraduate studies, the system had changed and I learned how to slide brittle squares of plastic into a mini projector in order to access the same information.

By the time I came to spend a year in a third university, in 1989, I sat down in front of a computer screen. My early adult years were set against the backdrop of a revolution I didn't know was happening. Now, I am, in the lingo, an 'immigrant'; without going anywhere, I have become a foreigner in the country of the computer. Dorothy has not gone to Oz: Oz has come to Dorothy. And, by an accident of history, I will never entirely be part of the future.

Poor Michael. Poor me. Surely this can only be a terrible handicap to a mother, when it comes to communicating with her fully naturalized-computerized children? Or perhaps not. Might it be both Michael's and my good fortune that I have found myself free-falling down the rabbit hole of history, one minute straining to get through the wrong-sized door, the next reaching as high as I can, but not high enough, for the antidote on the glass table? I am in the privileged if uncomfortable position of being on the cusp of something. This means that I can look both backwards and forwards in time. Can I start by pointing out to Michael the sort of books he most enjoys reading, the computer games he loves to play? Age of Empire, Age of Mythology, the Roman Mysteries, cartoon versions of the Greek myths, of the Odyssey, the Iliad and the Percy Jackson series in which the son of Poseidon is to be found combating evil in present day North America.

The popular culture my son is lapping up has, as its direct lineage, the civilizations of the Ancient Mediterranean. Both the languages he speaks (English and Italian) are intricately laced through with the meanings, metaphors and rhythms of thought of those 'dead' cultures. The counterpoint of these and all the other many cultures that make Michael what he is, and who he will become, create a rich music.

So what is this furious, dogged resistance of Michael's to learning Latin and Greek? A lot of it is about growing up: viscerally resisting an education system that bulldozes across the landscapes of childhood, formalizing myth into history, play into drudgery. He is right to be suspicious: the juggernauts of outmoded traditions and institutions flatten many children. Five years at the Liceo Classico strikes me as a sort of peculiarly protracted initiation rite. If you survive its brutality, then you come out an adult, able to face hard, tedious work and, perhaps, to turn it into something better and bigger. I wonder whether it is preferable to undergo five years of boredom interlaced with panic and despair than to live through a week in the jungle, having your body lacerated by the juice of poisonous plants.

In the meantime, Michael has his own take on the matter.

'I know what you would say about those dead languages, Mum,' he tells me some time into his relentless first term at the Liceo Classico. 'You'd say that if aliens landed on earth, they would communicate with us in ancient Greek. But you're wrong, because the nearest habitable planet is 500 light years from earth, so they will have been observing us in Tudor times, which means that what they'll actually say when they arrive is: "Hail, sire!" '

But, having accepted the spirit if not the accuracy of Michael's creative physics, this isn't right either: travellers in sixteenth-century Europe would, in fact, have used Latin as their lingua franca; a 'Hail, sire!' was much less likely to have been understood than the Roman greeting 'Salve!'

All of which goes to prove, once again, that history and time have wonderful ways of slipping sideways, backwards and forwards, and that Michael, when he finally comes face to face with his Martian, might have to start thinking it through all over again.

The historian Theodore Zeldin thinks that boredom has taken over from loneliness in the modern consciousness. I wish neither boredom nor loneliness on anyone, but mental repose and solitude are another matter. Turning back and trying to wade against the tide of history is a hopeless enterprise, just as being seduced by its great forward surge can also bring disaster, but I wonder if we could only harness as a metaphor and manifesto this ancient, improbable Venice, built such a long time ago, out of long dead necessities, to our *future* good?

There must be room in our vision of the future for a world of changing perspectives – where an individual can move from the virtual to the actual, from history to the present day; where, emerging from the maze-like networks of the internet, a child can come out into

the open and see, ahead, across space, that great white church and say
– 'Ah ...'

Technicals

WHEN MY WASHING machine breaks down, Oscar arrives. He is a
small, elderly man, in a perfectly laundered white shirt, trousers and
jacket and shining shoes. He moves in a fragrant cloud of aftershave
and brings with him his *tecnico* – the electrician – a young man with a
wry smile, whose clothes, though neat, are workers' clothes and, unlike
Oscar's, show some signs of use.

The two men edge gingerly into our narrow strip of kitchen. Having
examined the machine, the *tecnico* starts to explain to me why we will
need to get a new one. Oscar breaks in.

'Oh no. You need to speak with the landlord. The signora is renting
the house. And anyway, she is not Venetian.'

'All the same,' I smile, 'I still need a washing machine.'

Oscar smiles brightly, uncomprehendingly, back.

The new machine is to be delivered next week. The main landing
stage closest to our house is on the Grand Canal, which is a ten-minute
walk away. The machine will have to be unloaded from a boat and then
trundled to Calle del Vin on a trolley. Once at number 3460 it must be
transported up the four flights of stairs to our apartment. It will be a
small miracle of muscle power and logistics if this large piece of white
goods ever gets to our kitchen.

When the street door bell rings, I buzz in the delivery men. Then,
I open the door of the flat and wait. Many minutes later and still two
floors down, I hear the sounds of extreme effort: grunting and hard
breathing. Eventually, the gleaming new washing machine appears
around the corner, on the landing below, in the arms of the largest
human being I have ever seen. Helping him with the fancier footwork
is a second man, the size of a leprechaun.

When at last this unlikely couple manages to manoeuvre the
washing machine through our front door and into the kitchen, the big

man is a red mountain of fleshy, sweating effort. As they plumb it in, they chat away to me, but in such a dense Venetian dialect that I can only smile and nod and hazard a guess at what they might be saying.

Next, they drag the old machine into the narrow hall and leave it blocking the front door, in a growing pool of water that is dripping from the disconnected tube.

'All right,' they say. 'Goodbye, Signora,' and start off down the stairs.

'But,' I call at their disappearing backs, 'what about this?' – waving hopelessly at the abandoned machine – 'you're going to take it away, aren't you?'

The fat man turns around again and grins up at me from the landing below.

'Oh no, Signora. It only says: "consignment" on our instructions. That's your problem.'

And he turns his great, drenched back on me and stumps heavily away, his miniature side-kick skittering close behind.

I stand at the door for a second then sprint back into the flat to check the paperwork. There it is: 'previous appliance to be removed'. I leap into action, squeeze past the jettisoned washing machine in the hall, and race, three steps at a time, down the stairs and out into the street. I fly along the *calle*, dodging tottery old ladies and buggies and dogs, breathless, desperate, until I have almost reached the quay on the Grand Canal and see – thank God – the massive hulk of the delivery man and his scampering partner about to get back on their boat.

'Hey, hey!' I gasp, waving the form wildly at them, 'it says you have to take the old one away, too.'

The fat man registers neither surprise, nor irritation.

'Oh yes,' he says, glancing at the paper. 'All right then,' and turns back towards my house. It was, it seems, at least worth a try.

At the Friday market there is a stall run by farmers who bring their produce by boat from one of the market garden islands of the Venetian Lagoon. A heavily built man in his forties with a wide, mild, ingenuous face and a surprisingly high voice serves the customers and a smiling woman, perhaps his wife, works alongside him.

Sitting a metre or so behind the stall is another man, in his sixties, and strikingly like the younger man at front of house. He straddles a small, three-legged stool and has, next to him, a stack of crates filled with artichokes and a plastic washing-up bowl of water. He takes an artichoke from a crate and, with his sharp knife, quickly and efficiently pares the dark, stringy leaves from the tender lower part of the flower. Then he drops the cream disc of flesh into the clean water and throws the leaves into a bin.

Having spent years dutifully gnawing minuscule bits of artichoke flesh off woody leaves, in the French way, I relish this peremptory Italian rejection of all that nonsense, cutting to the quick and the best part of the plant.

The farmers from the island sell a limited number of vegetables – only those, in fact, that grow in their proper season, a few kilometres away from the city. Occasionally, they have something extra: heaps of sour, walnut-sized fruit that are, the younger man explains, a sort of plum. These clearly do not come from any kind of cultivated stock; they look like little, wild crab apples, and must have been gleaned from trees around the fields.

In the spring, they sell ungainly bunches of mimosa: masses of lovely, lollopy yellow heads, the stalks bound together with twigs. They will not sit up in any kind of container and shed their fluffy blooms within hours, but I buy them all the same.

There are often several people waiting to buy from the farmers, whose produce has been harvested that morning and carried the shortest of distances to market. But even if there is a long queue, the procedure remains the same: the fluty-voiced son and his smiling wife serve, while the father sits, legs planted wide apart, peacefully paring artichokes.

Once, soon after my arrival, I say to the son: 'So, you have a farm on the island?'

He looks at me, visibly surprised, and says: 'We *are* the island.'

Although we are standing and talking together in the market square, I see in that moment that this island farmer and I come from separate universes.

One day, when I am teaching English to a class of thirteen-year-olds at a local school, I ask them what their ambitions are. One boy, with a cocky smile, a slick of black hair and a satiny bomber jacket says:

'I want to be a taxi driver.'

'Why?'

'Because I like the water.'

It takes me, bred in London as I was, some moments to understand what on earth he could mean.

Thursday 15 December

IN THE MORNING, I need to do some shopping. It is cold outside and I rug up well in coat, hat, gloves and wellies and set off along the *calle*, pulling my pink flowery shopping trolley behind me.

The city is grey and tired. It registers nothing of the impending festivities: Christmas is always surprisingly absent from the streets of Venice. Walking along the *fondamenta* towards the boat stop, I slush through several inches of water and more is slopping up from the canal and running across the paving stones, like waves fanning out over the sand at the beach. Everyone in the *calle* is wading along very slowly, taking care not to splash water over the top of their boots. The *acqua alta* is high but not excessive and there is a strangely peaceful, slow motion feeling to it all; people are friendly and talkative, advising one another on the best routes to take from one place to another. It reminds me of those rare days in England when, after a heavy snowfall, there is the same good-humoured complicity of people united in the face of extreme weather. I stand and hesitate at a certain point, wondering which tack to take.

'If you come this way, Signora,' a young man says courteously, pointing diagonally across the flooding *fondamenta*, 'you'll keep on the high section of the pavement.'

I thank him and wade cautiously across.

In this lull before Christmas the city is as empty as it can be of tourists. The few remaining visitors are bundled up in warm clothes like everybody else and no more disposed to linger in the cold than the locals. The relief of these emptier streets is surprisingly intense. It feels good that we are all here for daily life and spared the elaborate weavings in and out between meandering holidaymakers. I need to go to the bookshop, but have not taken into account that it is at a very low point in the city which is always quick to flood. A steel barrier has been slotted into place on the lower part of the shop's doorway. These are used all over the city on ground floor premises, but it is clear that the proprietor was not sufficiently ahead of the game today because his shop is already full of water. I gather up my coat, shoulder my trolley, and high step over the barrier.

The scene I find inside reminds me of a famous photograph of Holland Park Library in London, taken immediately after the Blitz. In the ruined, rubbly shell of the bombed-out building, there are respectably homburg-ed and over-coated gentlemen browsing among the miraculously still-standing bookshelves. Here, in this Venetian shop, there is a gentler echo of that scene of devastation: in an atmosphere of quiet concentration, customers stand reading books or scanning the spines, in a good 30 centimetres of water. The bookshop has turned paddling pool, but business, surreally, serenely, carries on.

Back on the *fondamenta*, I wait for a boat to take me to the Co op. The cold is vicious in the sheltering *imbarcadero*. I am only going one stop, so once on the *vaporetto*, I stand outside on the open deck, my scarf wrapped around half of my face, against the biting cross-wind. The boat tips and roils as counter-currents buffet her bows. She grinds to a standstill on the other side of the canal and I pull my trolley off and wade along to the shops.

Inside the Co op it feels beautifully warm and bright. It is full of people, as if they can't quite bear to leave and brave the elements again and are lingering extra long among the fruit and veg. There is a holiday atmosphere in the queue to the checkout. A fat, elderly woman chats to me in dialect as we stand there. The low season and my full-to-bursting trolley make me a local. I smile and nod, as I always do when people talk to me in dialect. Since I usually manage to understand about half of what they're saying it feels like the safest course. It surprises me how much human interaction requires no more reply than a nod and a smile of agreement.

Back outside again, the waters have receded. On the stone paving of the *fondamenta*, there are streaks of seaweed jettisoned by the tide. Because, as usual, I have bought a lot, I drag my purchases home, with considerable effort, against the icy wind, along mud-slimed pavements. That is my morning in Venice, in December.

After lunch, I have business in Padua. A mere twenty minutes away in the car, Padua represents an hour and a half's travel for me today. First, there is the thirty-minute walk to the station through heavily gusting wind and pelting rain. For as long as I am in the narrow, high-walled *calles* I am reasonably protected from the elements, but as I come out into a wider wind-tunnelling *campo* my umbrella flips dramatically inside out and I am soaked by squalls of wind and rain.

Because it is a quarter of the price of the express train, I get a ticket for the more down-at-heel and graffitied *regionale* that stops at every single station. The train is full but warm, and I am settling down comfortably with my book for the forty-minute journey when I hear a suddenly raised voice at the other end of the carriage. A man is speaking; he has a strong Neapolitan accent and the Neapolitans' eloquent courtesy:

'Ladies and gentleman! Forgive this shameful request! I am on the train, but I have no ticket. I must get back to Naples, but they will throw me off at Padua. Please! A euro from fifteen of you and I will have enough to get home! Forgive me, I am ashamed to ask this! Please help, I beg you!'

Several people begin to rummage in their purses and the man steams up and down the carriage, garnering the money, thanking them in his booming, urgent voice. He has a battered, smudged face; a white bandage over one eye, jeans, dirty trainers.

'Thank you, Signora, you're very kind! Thank you, Signore! I thank you!'

The carriage is full of neatly dressed, subdued northerners. I am struck by how much mute generosity is shown to this needy and disturbed man. Then I hear another voice, further along the carriage:

'Ha, yes. Go on. You go back to Naples! The better for us. Then stay down there. We don't want you southerners here, understand?'

The speaker is a bullish-looking man in his sixties. He has on a smooth fedora and a dark-green jacket. The Neapolitan curses him harshly and thrusts past and out of the carriage.

An hour and a further bus ride later I arrive at my destination, a school in Padua, where I am going to do some English support teaching. I am early and sit down on the chair outside the secretary's office to wait for the head teacher. I am cold, wet and rather weary. The secretary comes out:

'Oh no, Signora. You must wait in the hall. You can't sit here.'

In the hall, there are no seats, so I stand, with my dripping umbrella at my feet. I can only assume that the apparently meaningless rules and regulations that criss-cross Italian public life give some meaning, some structure to *someone*, a sort of bureaucratic weft and warp. But I only wanted to sit down on that unoccupied chair.

After the midwinter darkness has fallen, I leave the school and head for the bus stop. There is already someone standing there, huddled under the bus shelter, the rain driving through the beam of the streetlight above her head. She is a young English woman who teaches at the school. When the bus arrives, we get in together and sit talking. She is from Hull, a tall, stout girl with a kindly, round face, long bleached hair and thick black-framed spectacles. She is wearing a fluffy white coat and over-sized Peruvian gloves, and she keeps pushing her spectacles back up her nose. She could not look less Italian and, to me, there is something comforting about her broad Yorkshire accent, her lack of vanity. In the warm, almost empty bus with its steamed-up windows we talk about England.

'I am the first person in my family to go to university. When I go home, people can get a bit sniffy. You know, I didn't have a baby by the time I was eighteen, like the other girls in my class. They say: "You're a bit posh, aren't you? Think you're better than us?" '

I don't know this girl from Adam; we come from very different parts of England and of English society, but she is none the less familiar to me and somehow, strangely, more *real* – though more real than what, I cannot say.

It is a relief to be talking in English in a public place, but *outside* Venice; to be foreign, but not one of the invading army. The few other people sitting nearby look up and register that we are not speaking their language, but without judgement. Only at moments like this, when I am away from Venice, do I realize how insidiously unhealthy it can be, living as an unwanted foreigner in a community that is under siege from the rest of the world.

Wind-battered, I get home after eight to find Lily in a state of hysteria, because she has just eaten some pasta made by Michael which contained a large chip of china. Freddie, oblivious to this drama, is busy emptying the cupboards optimistically in search of a top hat.

I soothe Lily, fob Freddie off with a rogue tweed cap, and have a man-to-man chat with Roland about making more of an effort at school. I then spend twenty minutes trying to explain to Michael, who is desperately studying for a history test, why knowing the difference between the fine details of romanesque and gothic architecture should even remotely matter to a thirteen-year-old boy.

Once they are all in bed, I leave the house for the last appointment of the day. The dark *calle* is still bitterly cold, but at least the rain has stopped and the high water has sunk back down. As I walk along the water front of the Zattere, a full moon brilliantly illuminates the white face of the church of the Redentore, across on the Giudecca. The wide Canal is like a dark glass filled to the brim. As I stroll through the empty streets I feel, for the first time today, calm. It is after ten and I am exhausted, but it is good to be out in the silent, bewintered city.

I arrive at my destination – the usual, anonymous door in a high wall. I ring the bell and the door snaps open. I pass through and find (Alice again) that I am in a garden. I follow a brick path through bare winter bushes and come to an open door spilling light. I climb the flight of shallow marble steps.

The meeting of the reading group is taking place in a big room where two curving sofas make an oval under an extravagantly sculpted gilt chandelier. Books are artfully heaped on tables and alongside the sofas. On one wall, there hangs an antique tapestry depicting a strangely unpopulated Arcadian landscape: there are trees and rivers and hills and fountains, but not a single living creature in sight. My friends, the members of the group, are sitting around, drinking wine in the candlelight. They are listening to a young woman who is reading aloud.

A little creakily, after so much trudging and huddling and battling against the elements, I sit down cross-legged on the floor, at the edge of the circle. I do not listen to a word the reader is saying, but the warm, subtle, open spaces around me, the intimacy of the group and its quiet unhurriedness, feel like heaven and it occurs to me that, at the end of it all, we might climb into the tapestry, like the children of Hamelin following the Pied Piper back into the hillside, and never come out again.

Iconic

IT IS NINE o'clock at night, the bells are tolling and we are wading to church. Piazza San Marco is a shallow, luminescent lake across which we must walk in order to reach the Basilica. Around all four sides of the great rectangular space lights shine and are reflected in the rising water. It is Christmas Eve and we are going to Midnight Mass which has, this year, been brought forward two hours because by midnight the waters will be impassable.

So far, so good: we are well within the territory of Venetian cliché: bells, lights, water and architectural wonders.

Inside the Basilica, the key notes are more prosaic: packed along pews, in the side aisles and leaning around the walls are hundreds of people wearing wellington boots. Rigged up to the marble pillars that line the nave are large flat screens relaying a close-up view of the priest and prelates conducting the Mass. Whether it's the boots or the screens, the atmosphere is neither hushed nor holy. A light steam rises

111

from the hundreds of damp bodies.

The service is being delivered in a strange mishmash of languages – Italian, Latin, French, German and English – and as it winds its way along, between chanting and intoning and song, much of the congregation is busy taking clandestine or not so clandestine photographs of the glorious mosaic ceilings. Different sensibilities are revealed here, but they are united in their need to immortalize the Immortal.

A little way into the Mass, a cameraman appears and walks up the central aisle. He is a strange, amphibious creature who seems just to have emerged from some post-apocalyptic swamp. He is wearing brown thigh-high waders, a dark woolly hat and a damp, sludge-green rain-jacket. He balances his bulky television camera on one shoulder and on his back he carries a rucksack, out of which protrudes a black umbrella. He wanders up and down the church, filming the people watching the film of the priests who are droning on, joylessly, up at the front.

The whole occasion has an entirely random feeling to it; there is a general air of distraction, what with the weather and the cameras and the fidgeting, shuffling congregation. What is most alive here, it strikes me, is the building itself: a dim, breathing presence that surrounds us like a sleeping beast, into whose leviathan belly we have entered and found caverns encrusted with blood and minerals.

The mosaics are all lit up tonight and the millions of gold tessellations glitter and merge, like the constellations of the Milky Way, so heaving with stars that no single point is visible any more, except in the brief glint of an individual star. Vaulted ceilings link one to the other and recede into shadowy distances of chapel and aisle. Ancient saints raise their flat hands in benediction. At the high altar the Pala d'Oro, the bejewelled treasure of San Marco, has been turned to face the body of the church. From where I sit at the back, it looks like a vast piece of gold bullion and is brutishly dazzling.

Everything is lapped and framed by the sea: panels of marble, each one different, swirling, rippling, flowing so that you feel you are swimming underwater, kicking idly along, your masked face down, following the maverick currents, the ridges of waving sand and the passing shadows.

Now, the bishop processes to the pulpit to give his homily and the people get to their feet, bulky in their winter clothes. In the exact moment that he begins his address, the high water siren starts to sound. First the miserable wartime wail; then the pips: one tone … up to the second … and a third. Now, no one is listening to the bishop, and everybody is wondering if they will get home dry as God causes his waters to cover the face of the earth.

The singing begins again and the inaudible words move like a slow and ungainly oral Mexican wave from corner to corner of the great church, with its many alcoves and inner spaces.

At last, the service is over and the chain-swinging priests pace solemnly away from the altar and down the aisle. Once they have gone, the welly-booted congregation begins its slow shuffle out towards the night.

The water is already creeping in through the main doors so the crowd has to edge its way along raised wooden walkways. We duck back into the Basilica to avoid this funereal catwalk and move against the flow of people, heading towards a side door.

We pass an altar where three Franciscan monks are kneeling in front of an ancient icon and praying intensely. The pink-cheeked virgin looks down on them, like a paper doll coloured lovingly by a little girl. Her sweet, two-dimensional face has a holiness and simple religiosity that is otherwise absent here tonight. Even the great building is wild and strange, somehow (should one say it?) pagan. Its aqueous marble and veins of deep gold are imbued more with the animus of the prehistoric cave and the Shaman than with Christianity.

I stop for a moment, moved by the stillness of these monks and the gently human image of divinity to which they pray.

Then, quite suddenly, the monk closest to the altar lifts his head, lowers his praying hands and, in a seamlessly elegant single movement, rises to his feet, whips from the brown folds of his robes a camera, and snaps the glowing icon.

PART 6: January

The Old Man and the Sea

'Those are pearls that were his eyes.'

SICK OF THE dog-shit-smeared streets of Venice, I take a *vaporetto* out to a distant island, on a frozen January morning. The world of the Lagoon is empty, the water torpid, and the boat moves through it like scissors searing through silk. Only light and the absence of light, water and air and movement figure here. I sit outside, at the back of the *vaporetto*, and feel my mind become cool and grey and old. Diving birds pierce the water with their needle beaks and the points multiply in circles of magical stitches, dimpling, replicating.

When the boat pulls up at the island quay only a few people get off, though even at this most benighted moment of the year nowhere associated with Venice is entirely without its ebb and flow of visitors.

I dawdle and let my fellow passengers go on ahead. I walk slowly along the pristine brick path that winds its way beside a canal, to the centre of the island. The savannah of reeds on either side of the path moves, even in the air deadened by cold, making subtle waves of dry, unmodulated sound.

On the island there is a solitary church, all that remains of a once populous settlement. In the space outside the main doors of this church – perhaps once a piazza, now a bowl of uneven, ragged grass

114

– there is a stall and I stop here for hot chocolate. A short way off, a group of tourists is huddled around a guide, as if for warmth.

'There are tours even at this time of year ...' I say to the woman who is preparing my chocolate.

'There are tours all through the year.'

'It wasn't like this last time I came here.'

'When was that?'

'Fifteen years ago perhaps ...'

'E! Cio!' she shrugs humorously in that way Venetians have of saying: well, there you are: I could have told you that everything goes to the bad.

'You should see it in the summer!' she adds, handing me the hot, soft plastic cup of thick chocolate.

Afterwards, I start off towards the church but then, on an impulse, turn to walk instead around the outside of the plain, brick building. Here, too, is another expanse of balding grass divided by a narrow path leading out towards agricultural land. I set off along the track, which is lined by high bushes of tamarisk sensing, but not seeing, the water close by.

I keep on until I reach a bridge spanning a fairly wide canal, which cuts between reed beds. I stop at the midpoint of the bridge and rest both hands on the rail. The wood feels slightly warm, though my breath plumes in the dank air. I watch bands of robber gulls tussling over a fish. The ripping flesh shows black, red and silver and the marauders tear it into shreds in their orgy of greed, then reel out from the fracas, like white petals scattering.

A bloody drama of survival and social life is being enacted in this serene world of sky and glassy water. The rustling chorus of reeds is neither animal nor elemental. Standing here, I understand the ancient thought that, blended into stems and leaves, there is another invisible life which inhabits a mythical space between flesh and blood and sap. This is the life of dryads, nymphs, fairies, sprites.

When a hand touches my arm I am not even surprised. Standing beside me, there is a very small, very old man.

'Beautiful, isn't it?' His grin is gap-toothed; he is wrinkled like a

115

smoked kipper; his muddy eyes are eager. I smile back and nod.

'I'm eighty-five,' he chuckles. 'Think of that! My sons look after the vines now. And my grandsons.' He touches my arm again. 'Come. I'll show you something.'

I follow the old man over the bridge, through the flanking reeds, into a flat expanse of vineyard.

'Come!' He crab-scuttles ahead of me, neat and quick and creaky, along a row of vines. We arrive at a wooden hut, streaked and darkened by rain. He pushes the door open and beckons me in.

The shed is lined from floor to low ceiling with shelves; they are packed with tools, bundles of magazines, balls of string, loops of rope. The only light comes from one porthole of a window. The old man bends and pulls forward an empty oil can. 'Sit!' he says and hauls out a three-legged stool for himself.

But he does not sit down and begins instead to rummage around at the back of the shed where he finds a large unlabelled bottle and two glasses. He wipes them clean with a rag and then places them on an upturned wooden crate. Then, having unscrewed the bottle cap, he pours an inch of red wine into each small glass. He hands me one, settles himself on the stool, and raises his glass.

'Saluti, Signora!' he wheezes and drinks.

The wine is strong and vinegary; the rough alcohol warms me.

Quickly now, the old man puts down his glass and stands up again. 'Shall I show you what I found?'

Again, he pokes around in his elaborate filing system of shelves, every so often pulling out a parcel wrapped in newspaper, which he lays on the bench beside him.

'I've dug these up over the years, or sometimes, when I was fishing, I found them in the Lagoon. Once, a long time ago, there was a great city here, a lot of people. These things come from that time.'

With the slow precision of those who work with their hands and whose intellectual life is expressed physically, he unwraps the parcels one by one. He brings out many fragments of pottery: a blue curve of renaissance majolica, patches of ancient pavement, gobbets of gold-leafed mosaic, deep glazes holding terracotta like meat in aspic. He shows me dented silver cups and archaic cutlery: fork prongs undulating like tentacles, a bone knife handle.

I take each new treasure and turn it over and admire it. There is a rhythm and an enchantment in the slow examination of these bits and pieces of history, in the mild intoxication of the wine and the serendipity of being here at all, in this hut, among the vines and the rushes.

The old man too is relishing the unlikely theatre and his captive audience of one. He is like an aged Caliban, tranquil now on his island, long ago abandoned by Prospero, the court and princely knowledge. Rickety on his rickety stool, fond, nostalgic, gleeful, he handles his master's relics: the beautiful, broken, glittering and useless memorabilia of the past.

'But this – you must see!' he says suddenly, as if deciding on something there and then, and, climbing on to his stool, he reaches up to the highest shelf for a parcel the size of a melon. He brings it down with extreme care.

'Ecco!' he says.

From its newspaper sarcophagus he produces a sphere of silver filigree which seems to have been spun from a living filament of silk. It is a renaissance censer; the silver chain lies slack over his brown hands, as he holds the ball up, offering it to the meagre light from the window. The pallid winter sun barely penetrates, but the censer seems to hold an inner illumination, which runs like electric currents around the sweeps and curves of palely shining metal to its spiralling core.

Now, the old man cradles the sphere back in towards him as though still unable to believe that he possesses such a marvel. He pulls the sleeve of his jacket into his fist and rubs at the metal which begins to gleam darkly.

'I was catching crabs,' he looks at me keenly. 'It was buried in mud.'

He lays the censer back in its newspaper and wraps it tightly, before stowing it away again, on the top shelf.

Then he quickly rewraps some of the pottery pieces, putting them into a plastic carrier.

'I can't give you that,' he nods in the direction of the censer, 'but these are for you.' He hands me the bag. I stand up to take it, formally.

'Grazie,' I say.

Then, on a whim, mildly intoxicated, perhaps inappropriate, I lean down and kiss the old man on his leather cheek and run for the last *vaporetto*.

Three, or Is Dead Beautiful?

YOU CAN SPOT it a long way off: it is a sleeker beast than its sisters, the *vaporetti* Numbers One and Two, because it does not bristle with passengers, leaning over the side, pointing, photographing, gazing or gawping at the slipping-by splendours of the Grand Canal. It is also differently coloured, altogether more subdued. As it pulls up to a stop, the people who step swiftly off the Number Three are uniformly dressed in black, brown, grey, dark green and blue, but never – ever – the slippery white of leisure wear; never the fluorescent orange or acid yellow rain-jackets emblazoned with swashbuckling names like Everest, Trekker, North Face, Arctic, Sahara.

Despite the more muted tones, there is a relaxed, almost holiday atmosphere aboard the Number Three. Strangers pass comments to each other about the weather or the state of the water; the *marinaio* has time to joke with the passengers as he throws the rope and ties the boat up to the landing stage, before drawing back the barrier and letting them off. Only aboard the Number Three can a Venetian be more or less certain of being understood by the person sitting next to him; there is a feeling of being at home, of closing the door on the outside world, of being among friends. This is because everyone on board the Number Three does, actually, live in Venice.

'No tourists!' the *marinaio* calls out as the Three comes up to a stop, 'Season ticket holders only!' and visitors to the city fall back, confused, accepting or irritated, as the residents stream past them on to the boat. The Number Three is always pleasantly uncrowded; in high tourist season, the old, the disabled, those with buggies or toddlers or a lot of shopping, let the One and Two, bursting with tourists, go by, and wait instead for the calm of the Three.

Within weeks of its inauguration, I overhear a man in the street referring to someone as having a head as empty as the Number Three; it has already become part of the proverbial landscape.

But it is not only colour and numbers that distinguish the passengers on the Three; it is a subtle but unmistakable difference of purpose that infuses every pore of the people who use it. Tourists are visibly mystified when the *marinaio* does not even stop to look at individual passes, and yet suddenly, unaccountably, prevents certain people from getting on to the *vaporetto*. But to those of us who are hurrying to school, or university, or the market, or work, it is perfectly clear that the man on the right is a tourist, while the man on the left is going to fetch his son from nursery. The *marinaio* does not need to see their tickets to know that. Why? Because human beings on holiday are radically different from human beings who are negotiating their way through the myriad small hurdles of daily life. It is as if the billions of atoms of which we are made become somehow more compacted when there is a job to be done, so that we exude purpose like a powerful scent – even, somehow, look different.

Holidaymakers inhabit a different skin; they are, above all else, in no hurry. The long day ahead contains no appointments, commitments, decisions or duties; all they have to do is eat and sleep and enjoy themselves as much as they possibly can. In this happy state of no-responsibility the body, so often tensed for action, relaxes. Their aura is unmistakably looser, their pace slower: they amble, pause to admire, hesitate about which direction to take, turn back to pass comment to a companion. They are, in a way, infantilized because they have been relieved of all the pressure to keep up to speed, on track or any of the other heart-racing metaphors favoured by Western culture in the world of work.

When we become tourists, we become childlike in our faint uncertainty: away from our known environment, we are not entirely confident, might be downright bamboozled. Banal details of life become major obstacles: how to navigate a transport system or match the look of a shop with what it is selling. As tourists, we are never precisely sure what is going on around us. This is both freeing and perplexing.

None of this need be a problem: people have always travelled in foreign places, briefly inhabited and observed them, moved on. The difference in Venice, though, is all down to numbers.

There is a pharmacy in a central Venetian *campo* with a digital sign displayed in the window. This records, defiantly, heartbreakingly, from month to month, the current resident population of the city. The officially registered population of Venice is about 60,000. This is around a third of what it was sixty years ago. Approximately 16.5 million tourists visit the city every year.

Often, I hear visitors say, in smugly pragmatic vein, 'Yes, but without the tourists, Venice wouldn't survive.'

And I want to scream: 'DO THE SUMS! This is not a healthily balanced ecosystem! Make the leap: understand that for every one person who lives in this place, there are approximately another 267 extra (and extraneous) tourists milling around her as she attempts to move through the city.'

'The population of Venice is about the same as that of Hereford. Think how it would be if you lived in a medium-sized town like this and every time you left the house to go to the shops, to school, to work or to visit a friend, you found yourself wading through seas of day trippers (about 12.5 million of the total annual number of visitors to Venice come for the day only). These people have no investment in your town; they have come here merely to look, pay, leave. Every way you turn, there are people taking photographs of your washing, your children, your shopping trolley, your dog. Imagine what it might feel like to be condemned to a lifetime as walk-on parts in a picturesque stage set which just happens to be your home as well. Giorgio tells me how, one Saturday afternoon in June, he left his house in a quiet corner of the city, with the intention of going to see his mother on the other side of the Grand Canal.

'I got to the Strada Nuova,' he smiles gently, 'and I looked at all those hundreds of people streaming past and I just thought, "I can't handle it" and I turned round and went back home.'

Lilli jokes grimly: 'I live in the industrial zone of Venice.' Her house is, in fact, near to Piazza San Marco which 'processes' tens of thousands of tourists a day.

The extreme numbers of drifting visitors affect the rhythm of the place. A bridge becomes impassable because twenty people have sat down to eat sandwiches on its steps; a narrow street is barely navigable for a person in a hurry when others are stopping in front of shop windows, passing the long, lovely, empty holiday hours of the day. And this bridge, this narrow street which almost anywhere else in the world would be pretty by-ways, are in Venice major thoroughfares linking one part of the city to another so that the easy flow of everyday life is chronically inhibited. As a result, some areas have become deserts: places where the only people who go there by choice are tourists.

What puts Venice in peril (may already have done for it) is that its economy is hugely, disproportionately dependent on a single commodity: tourism. This means that the vast majority of people who walk its streets are in some way dependent on that system, either for their livelihood, or as its consumers. In this monoculture people are constantly re-enacting the same limited roles: as purveyors or consumers of the city as museum or playground. Venice becomes, merely, a transient place. But what any city needs to survive are the people who stay, the people who put down roots and nourish it and hold it together and give back to it a lasting diversity.

Much of Venice is now, you might say, chronically deforested and swathes of the city are effectively desert because real life is no longer taking place in them. There is nothing to make them fertile: as the hardware shops and butchers and shoe-menders and bakeries shut down; as the inhabitants are driven out by landlords greedy for the high tourist rents. Mask outlets and pizza vendors and tacky souvenir stalls usurp all other shops, and the many, varied transactions that should take place in daily life are fatally limited.

A city is impoverished at the profoundest of levels when the only exchanges taking place are between strangers and are all to do with the transitory experience of a short visit, with four limited goals: to look, to sleep, to feed and to buy. Of course there is still the beauty – there's always that. But what kind of beauty is barren? Is dead beautiful?

Holidays are delightful things, but they are only ever brief exeats from the real business of living. Relationships, creative endeavour, community enterprises do not happen on daytrips. And if Venice becomes nothing more than one giant daytrip destination it will perish – will, well and truly, have become that exquisite, empty backdrop over which we coo and gush, on to which we project our fantasies and desires. People walk the streets, marvel at the buildings and go. The only thing they leave behind is their cash. Even the most lavishly appreciative, the most sensitively self-effacing tourist can give only money back to Venice.

Quick fixes do not bear lasting fruit in any area of human activity. The indiscriminate handing out of resources is only ever of dubious benefit in the long run. A food parcel does not put down roots and bear next year's harvest. Where there is no possibility of a relationship between giver and receiver, the recipient fast becomes dependent on a one-way flow of gifts. The complex internal structures of a community soon atrophy, because all its attention is directed outwards, to the external sources upon which it has become dependent. In a community where all that counts is personal gain from a single source of income, individuals stop investing in a multifaceted and complex society; they stop diversifying into relationships or activities and become single-mindedly focused on just one aspect of life: the getting and using of a sole commodity.

Human society is characterized by culture. Culture is the product of multiple endeavours and enterprises. Dependence removes the possibility of genuine dialogue and mutual benefit, and you are left with a group of people, heads upturned, beaks agape, gasping for the next worm, like a row of squawking fledglings in a nest.

In Venice, the wealthy hoteliers, the purveyors of knick-knacks, the dodgy politicians, the restaurateurs, the taxi boat drivers who winter in the Caribbean on the takings of the summer season, might be surprised at being compared with the starving masses or a nestful of clamouring hatchlings, but there is a parallel to be drawn here and it is my friend Pisana, a secondary school teacher, who first brings it to my attention.

We are talking about the sad straits in which much of Venice finds itself, about the death of its communities, the paucity of municipal support for enterprises other than tourism, the overwhelming influence of money-grabbing business interests and individuals who know that pimping the Whore Venice to the ever greater and grosser incursions of tourists is their quickest way to a fortune.

'But surely,' I say, 'there's another scenario: a future in which the city can become a place of artistic and artisanal excellence again and a cultural centre where people are able to live on a small, environmentally sustainable and creative scale?'

She shrugs. 'You know,' she says sadly, 'when I ask the kids in my class what they want to do when they leave school, they all say the same thing: we want to own a hotel or run a restaurant.'

Could it be that just as the son of the drought-stricken African farmer no longer needs to remember the lore of the land – the rhythms of preparation and planting and harvesting – because a sack of grain will always – probably – arrive from somewhere else, these well-heeled Venetian children, growing up in a mono-economy, have lost sight of what is most valuable and ultimately productive? Belonging to a community that is rich and yielding, that takes them forward into new adventures, rather than round and round on the merry-go-round of acquisition and consumption? If children have no imagination, how can they imagine the future or the past? And why should they give a damn about it? That is when Venice – not the stones, but the community – is no longer merely in peril, but extinct.

Meanwhile, like parents looking abstractedly on as the children devour the party tea and lay waste to the house, the Venetians sometimes seem to me perversely uninterested in the delights that surround them. In those early months after my arrival, I at first think that what most distinguishes me from the natives is not my dress or my body language, but the fact that I cannot resist, as I step over a bridge, the impulse to glance sideways and drink in a shaft of creamy sunlight across dull-green water, the quirky angle of a corner, a slash of crumbling red stone seen through pink stucco.

But I am wrong. Over time, I am touched to see, as the *vaporetto*

Number Three floats by, that there are often people sitting in the outside seats at the back of the boat. On the Numbers One and Two, no resident of the city would bother to do anything other than head straight into the cabin, find a place and get to their destination, leaving the outside seats and the view for the eager, greedy, jostling visitors. But on the Number Three, where layers upon layers of tourists have been miraculously peeled away, you can see Venetians themselves leaning on the bar, staring dreamily, curiously, appreciatively, at the wonders of their city; or sunning themselves at the back, reading a book and quietly relishing their home, as they float along the Grand Canal to work.

RIP: Less than one year after the triumphant inauguration of the Number Three (all aboard the press! The flashing cameras! The politicians!), I return to Venice after a holiday and find that the line is no longer for the exclusive use of residents; it is, indeed, soon to be cut altogether. It is not economically viable. Perhaps the authorities knew this would happen, but thought they could curry a few more votes by throwing a temporary sop to the exhausted Venetians.

Baba Yaga

'O, reason not the need: our basest beggars
Are in the poorest thing superfluous'

(*King Lear*, 2.4. 291–305)

'Bury me standing, I've spent all my life on my knees'

(Gypsy saying)

ON ONE OF the bridges that I cross several times a day as I walk to school and back with my children, an old gypsy woman begs for money. I say 'old', though I struggle to pinpoint her actual age.

Nothing about her appearance or her behaviour gives me a clue as to who or what she really is.

For a start, the woman is dressed in the costume of fairy tale. She wears a dark headscarf knotted under her chin and a shapeless dress in some equally drab material. An apron is tied around her waist, and draped over her shoulders is a triangular fringed shawl. None of her clothing seems to have been touched by industrial dye: the rough cloth might have been dipped in berry juice, or boiled nettles or onion skins or mud. Her brown skin is profoundly creased, but somehow smooth at the same time, and she has few teeth.

She kneels, bent forward in supplication over an empty sardine can. Propped against her knees there is a small card with a highly tinted image of the Madonna. The cerulean blue of the Virgin's shawl, her pious upward look, her hands, palm to palm in ecstatic supplication, make the old beggar woman who, from time to time, also gazes skywards, in wrinkled parody of the picture, to my eyes, both a fraud and an alien.

For hours on end, she rocks back and forth and intones in a harsh monotone 'Buono … Buono … Buono …' And although her pose is one of dereliction and dependency, she commands attention. Her grating incantation is compelling, sinister even, and I half wonder if she has left her broomstick around the corner; if, at the end of the day, she will pull her shawl tight about her shoulders, retrieve her besom, and soar into the gathering darkness, the wind carrying her back to some forest faraway to the east, where her chicken-legged hut whirls and scampers randomly among the trees like that of the legendary Russian witch, Baba Yaga.

The reality is, of course, quite different. In the early morning, as the commuters flood into the city from Mestre, many of them to service the tourist industry, so too do the beggars, that same industry's underbelly and underclass. Little huddles of women arrive, some carrying babies, all bundled in the same shapeless peasants' garb. They talk among themselves as they walk briskly up the Strada Nuova. They are smaller than everyone else, tougher, uglier, harder and utterly separate.

Throughout the day, these same women are to be found stationed around the city, solitary now, and on their knees; prone, bent double and begging. Sometimes they moan or groan in pain and supplication. Once positioned on their pitch, they each assume a particular expression – either of grief or suffering or resignation or despair – which stays fixed on their faces like a mask for all the long hours of their begging day.

Although they rarely look directly at the passers-by, they can be seen appraising with perfect acuity whoever is approaching, a discrete glance telling them whether it is worth rocking harder for the next punter.

Sometimes, a policeman will walk past and move them on, joking: 'Come on, it's no good for your knees to stay on that cold stone all day,' and the gypsy women with their angry eyes do not answer, as they heave themselves up, shoulder their rucksacks and move around the corner, to wait until the policeman has gone, so that they can go back and resume their extraordinary show of imploring desolation.

One aged crone shuffles, shoeless, around Campo Santa Margherita, right angled over her stick, her begging tin extended in one crabbed hand, her gaze, always, downwards. It is her saggy-stockinged feet that most strike me; I try to imagine how it feels to shuffle like that, on those unforgiving paving stones, all day long. I notice that she sifts through the lively, pacy crowds in small, apparently random circling movements. When I look harder, I see that there is a logic to her progress, as though she were moving across the *campo*, very slowly, with a metal detector.

I can only imagine that these women are getting at least some reward for their efforts, though I very rarely see anybody stop to drop coins in their tins. Up until now, I have never given the woman on the bridge money either. But why should I, a person of liberal beliefs, who considers herself compassionate towards those less fortunate, react so uncharitably to this particular beggar?

Perhaps the answer lies in that very liberalness. Could it be precisely because the gypsy beggar has no place in the model of a liberal, secularized modern world that she does not touch a modern 'liberal' conscience? The image she presents of highly formalized, destitute supplication does not move me because, like the schmaltzy image of the Virgin in whose name she is begging, the old woman belongs to a culture to which I cannot connect. Despite her passive pose, there is about her a kind of fierceness. Nothing in my culture has prepared me to understand this combination of strength and weakness in the context of begging, and because I cannot reconcile the two elements, I feel her, viscerally, to be dishonest. I may be completely wrong in this, but in my culture pride and submission are not compatible: where I come from, only the utterly destitute – which is to say those destitute in mind as well as circumstance – resort to begging.

In Britain, we do not admit to a model of begging because we refuse to accept the idea of a class of institutionalized destitutes. Destitution can only be a terrible accident, or a sign of social breakdown. For obvious reasons, we refuse to accept either of these as anything other than exceptions to the rule: a blip in the pursuit of a greater good.

The grim-faced, talkative little bands of beggar women who stride into Venice every morning belong to another world altogether. The gypsy woman on the bridge has none of my pseudo-liberal hypocrisy: she is under no illusions about wealth and poverty and knows that she is a beggar and that she must therefore enact the part of beggar, just as any of us enact certain roles in our work. In doing this she is consciously placing herself within a social structure, slotting into the predesignated role of beggar.

This does not make of her anything less (or more) than a beggar, so why is it that I am able to give money to the red-eyed addict in a London underpass and not to this tiny, gnarled, knowing grandmother, on her knees in the street?

When I see a homeless drunk on the streets of London, I recoil from his visible degradation, but I am also compelled to empathize with him. My sense of social responsibility is not fuelled by religious belief, but by a conviction that here is another being with whom I share my humanity. I think that I have a notion of how he has arrived at this tragic point and I pity him accordingly, from the bottom of my selective heart. He and I belong to the same social structure; I am safe in it, he has drifted to its hopeless nether regions; there, but for the grace of God, go I. Bad luck, bad genes or bad governance have forced him into this place and I recognize these forces and believe that there is a way out for him ... possibly ... maybe ...

Unlike the drunk, the gypsy beggar does not consider herself as having drifted off the social map; on the contrary, she has a distinct place in it. Her job is begging and she commutes into Venice to beg. This does not make her a fake or a thief. She is part of a social structure in which begging for alms has its place; it is an ancient culture in which the moral appeal of beggars to the wealthy is based on religious obligation and the hope of buying a place in heaven:

'For alms are but the vehicles of prayer'
(John Dryden)

In begging for 'good, good, good', the picture-postcard image of the Virgin propped against her knees, the old woman on the bridge is telling us that the support of the poor is both a religious imperative and a social duty. What I must face up to is this: the fact that she is begging within a social structure does not make her situation any less desperate, nor does it mean that I should care for her any less.

And so, confused and uneasy, I resort to the child's eye imagery of the gypsy beggar as a witch. I do this because I can place her nowhere except in storyland – a generic, mythical figure. People like her don't have a place in my conscious, practical life, because I come from a society which is overwhelmed by the cult of the individual.

What motivates me to give away my money is the recognition of another individual and our common humanity. I am not moved by religious duty or belief, or by any kind of investment in a social hierarchy that makes some people into beggars for alms. I am motivated by guilt, by pity, by fear, by cod psychology. The waters are muddy. But when it comes to this muttering medieval mendicant on the bridge, a refugee from unknown lands to the east, I have no such difficulty and I sail past her daily, as though she were, indeed, a ghost in a parallel universe.

If the fishermen on the Giudecca, or that aged farmer on the lagoon island, provide me with a comforting cliché of the old ways, a pleasant nostalgia for the 'authentic', the gypsy beggar does not. One morning, as we hurry over the bridge to school, always late, always bounding two steps at a time, she is there as usual: Virgin at her knee, babushka headscarf, sardine can.

'Look at her!' Freddie shouts indignantly. 'I won't give money to her!'

And what can I say to him? 'Oh reason not the need! Would you, my boy, choose to spend your whole life on your knees?'

Because all that this secular, materialistic six-year-old sees is a beggar talking loudly on her mobile phone.

Giardino di Merda

THERE ARE HIDDEN gardens all over Venice. In January, when the city is at its stoniest, I might be walking down a narrow, grey *calle* and find myself suddenly engulfed in a cloud of rich perfume. Behind high walls, a gaunt witch hazel is in bloom – the little white flowers seeming to have been stuck along the naked branches and fiercely exuding summer into the cold, dead air.

In April, wisteria plays a similar trick, clambering over the walls and pouring down the other side to brush the heads of passers-by with purple blooms and thick, sweet scent.

The land birds of Venice nest in these gardens too. Sometimes I hear the trill of a blackbird and look up to see the little yellow-eyed creature perched on the top of a wall. And there are the plaguing mosquitoes too, lurking among the trees. Out at the back of the island of the Giudecca, on the edge of the South Lagoon, there are a number of grand, private gardens. Trees and climbing plants loll over brick and drift the tips of their leaves in the still water. You can see this only from a boat and, even then, you can only guess at the luxuriance of fig trees and roses, jasmine and willow tangling in there.

Of course, having a garden in Venice is a privilege. Often enough, people have bits of outside space attached to their houses – backyards, strips along the side of a building – but whether you can persuade any plant life to take root in these shady pockets is another matter. One afternoon, while we are waiting for our children to come out of school, Federico tells me about his 'garden', a small dank yard that never sees the sun.

'I was woken up at dawn last week. I heard this loud shouting coming from the back of my house. I was half asleep, but I went out on to the terrace to see what was happening and I found this drunken tramp lunging around down there. So I said, "Hey! What are you doing?" Well, he climbed back over the wall, cursing and swearing, and disappeared.

'Then, this morning, I heard the noise again and I found the same man crashing around out there and he looked up at me and yelled:

' "Oy! You! Signore with the shit courtyard!" '

Federico looks at me, laughing.

'You see what I mean? It really is a dump, even he knew that. Even in that state!'

I dream of having a garden in Venice, but only under certain circumstances. Maria Grazia has a large garden – full of mature trees and with a big, undulating lawn where generations of her children, grandchildren, and now great-grandchildren, play. It seems like an unimaginable luxury in this city of narrow streets and stone public spaces, but when I tell her how jealous I am, she smiles wryly.

'I call it the amphitheatre,' she says and gestures at the surrounding buildings. That's when I notice the tens of windows overlooking the garden from every side. Nothing that you do or say here could possibly go unobserved.

The courtyard garden of my neighbour Signora Zambon has distinct shades of the prison yard: the walls are so high and the surrounding buildings so beetling that for most of the day three-quarters of this brick cube is cast in shadow. There is a meagre patch of grass in the middle, which struggles to survive against all the odds. Grass can usually be counted on to tell you what a place is really like, underneath it all: the grass of Venice is rough and dry; it is, of course, dune grass, sea grass.

Signora Zambon spends much of her time in this garden. She is a dry, thin little woman, always dressed in a cardigan and pearls, even when she's getting her hands dirty with the big sacks of soil, the plants and pots that are delivered at regular intervals and stacked up in the communal entrance hall, before being hulked out back.

She has planted jasmine in the sunny part of the courtyard and it appears to be flourishing, but it is, for the most part, difficult to see where all that money and time has gone. Well, I think, most gardens tend to be like that, and anyway Zambon is not to be downcast: Zambon has a dream. She confesses it to me one day, as we pass on the staircase.

'I go to bed at night with the David Austin rose catalogue. There is nothing like it in Italy. I would like to fill my garden with English roses.'

I think of English roses in their English places: the white snow-storms of Kiftsgate; the heavy, odorous velvets staggering over village walls; smatterings of Dog Rose, tunnels of pink petals among the cobnuts, arcading hidden lanes.

'I can only grow roses in the pots on my *terrazza*,' she shakes her head mournfully; it is the nearest she can ever get to her dream, but still she won't relinquish David Austin. Even Signora Zambon smiles at this.

I begin to think about people who, despite where they actually are, dream of being somewhere and something else altogether. In the Signora's case, she may in fact be in the right place, but a few hundred years too late. The palazzo in which we both live was once famed for its beautiful garden. This dank, overhung courtyard is all that remains. I wish that for the shy, wary Zambon the clocks of Tom's Midnight Garden could chime thirteen and she might find herself strolling through the scented gardens of the Marcellani, in the cool night air.

PART 7: February

Village Fete

IT IS A dull February morning and a huge crowd has packed into Piazza San Marco and the Piazzetta, the space between the Doge's Palace and the waterfront looking out over the Basin of San Marco.

I am standing with my four children on the edge of this great crush.

'OK,' I say, 'link hands!' and we start to wriggle our way through, finally coming to a halt beneath the bell tower of San Marco, the campanile.

Strung over our heads and stretching from campanile to palace there is a thick wire. Dangling from its highest point, at the top of the campanile, are six massive, three-dimensional, white letters:

A-N-G-E-L-O.

When the great bronze men on the clock tower step forward and hammer out the twelve strokes of midday on the side of the bell, the so-called Angel of the Carnival will, we are told, fly down this zip wire and land effortlessly on the balcony or *loggia* of the Doge's palace – a fleet spirit, an Ariel, to inaugurate the Venetian Season of Misrule.

Every year, a celebrity of some kind or other performs what sounds like a not inconsiderable feat; this year, the Angel is a rapper, of whom I have never heard.

Now, the hammers are striking the bell and everyone is craning for a first glimpse of the Angel. Silence settles over the Piazza. Then, creakingly, the zip wire begins to move and the giant letters joggle slightly, then start to slip, rather jerkily and very slowly, downwards.

Now at last we can see the Angel. He is straddling the O, hands gripped tight around the wire from which it is suspended, his legs dangling in space. He is a large man, in a sparkly, white suit; even at this distance, he is visibly ill at ease.

The crowd cheers and the Angel cautiously raises one arm in salute. He and his letters continue to move clumsily, falteringly, down the wire, like an ancient ski lift in operation for the last time.

This is not the circus spectacular I had envisaged: the slick, horizontal swoop from campanile to *loggia*, and I am not the only one among the crowd to register surprise, albeit for a different reason. The people around me greet the Angel's appearance with amazement:

'Ma! E nero!' – 'But – he's black!'

This is the conspicuous official face of the opening of Carnival. Specially laid-on *vaporetti* with names like *Arlecchino* and *Colombina* can be seen steaming purposefully up the Grand Canal towards San Marco, where more and more tourists are being unloaded into the already heaving Piazza. Here, dramatically masked and enrobed individuals are striking mannequins' poses for the photographers – they are faceless and nameless celebrities for one day. From this point, thousands of visitors will soon set off around the city in search of Carnival happenings, both real and imagined.

These days, Carnival is not a Venetian festival; it is a recent revival of the old tradition, designed to squeeze yet more money from the insatiable tourists and is, as far as I can see, universally disliked by the inhabitants of the city. It goes on for days and has no real centre or purpose, but is a sprawling, random spread of events, among which tourists wander aimlessly in ridiculous masks.

For Venetians, Carnival is a another example of their perennial, nightmarish problem: somebody has organized an enormous party in your backyard but it's not your party and you don't know any of the guests. All you want to do is get on with your daily life in peace, but all around you there are millions of strangers doing just the opposite.

Not surprisingly, there is a mass exodus of residents from the city during these joyless festivities.

Still, as ever, real Venice clings on valiantly like a tenacious little limpet. On this first day of the Carnival and at the same time as the big, tacky public show, there is another, smaller and genuinely Venetian event taking place, nearby and on the water. The various rowing clubs of the city have gathered in the Basin of San Marco and are taking their own Carnival procession back *down* the Grand Canal, against the rising tide of tourists converging on the Piazza.

Earlier this morning, Jane and I decorated her lovely wooden boat, the prawn-tailed *sanpierota*, with strings of cotton flags and balloons. We have filled it with six children and two adults, all of whom are dressed up in hastily cut and stuck masks and headdresses. Jane is at the back, steering in a large Mad Hatter's top hat, and I am rowing *prua* (at the front), in a black nylon Batman cloak I found in the dressing-up box, and a gold mask that covers my whole face so that I am having a certain amount of difficulty in breathing even before I begin rowing a heavy boatload of people up the Grand Canal. We are a motley and cheerful crew as we join the string of thirty Venetian rowing boats of various sizes and shapes bobbing about in the little waves of the *bacino*.

The only close encounter between these two Carnival events takes place as the boat club rowers pass under the Accademia Bridge. Here, hundreds of tourists lean on the wooden rail and photograph us for all they are worth. What perhaps they cannot fully understand is that, moving under the famous bridge, processing between the venerable and fantastical palaces of the Grand Canal, is a small, waterborne village fete.

One boat, a *topo* is packed with people in crepe paper octopus hats, the multi-coloured tendrils falling over their shoulders. In another, a band of merrily un-PC cannibals are dancing to Bob Marley, blacked-up like minstrels, with woollen dreadlocks and crepe paper grass skirts over purple nylon tracksuits. A large *batelo* is crewed by six hefty men in blond wigs and Ugly Sister finery. They manage to row the whole length of the Grand Canal without smiling once.

On another boat, a wooden frame has been erected and then

lavishly draped with plastic vines and plastic oranges and lemons. Under this lopsided Bacchic pergola four fat, bearded men in aprons are busily frying fish in a cauldron, precariously balanced on a single gas ring. As the Carnival flotilla goes by, the four cooks use long slatted spoons to dredge up the fish from the spitting oil. They drop it into cones of white paper, which they fold shut and then lob across the water into our outstretched hands.

'Vino?' they shout and we lean over the edge of our boat towards them, holding out our plastic cups, precariously, across the water. From unlabelled bottles they lustily slug red wine in our direction – half of it reaches the cups, half slops into the Grand Canal.

Because there are so few bridges over the Canal and so few points of public access to the water's edge, this procession has few witnesses. The atmosphere down here at water level is friendly, informal, local and light-hearted – not much different, really, from any Sunday after-noon fancy-dress parade in any other village in Europe.

Dressing Up

EARLY MORNING IS the only time of day in Venice when you can be certain that the ratio of tourists to residents will be weighted in the residents' favour. It is, for me, the most magical time in any city; there is a sleep-tousled, unguarded, good-naturedness in the early morning streets that you find at no other hour of the day. In Venice this is more starkly the case than anywhere else simply because as the morning advances, the balance of tourists and residents undergoes a violent destabilizing swing, to the point where the life you observe on the streets after, say, 10 a.m., is in no way guaranteed 'authentic' and is much more likely to consist of the few limited transactions in the rep-ertoire of tourism: food, souvenirs, sightseeing, food again, and so on.

Every morning, I walk with my children across the wide *campo* that runs along one side of the church of the Frari. In the convoluted Venetian world of narrow alleyways, this space allows a fine opening of perspectives and reveals the great brick church silhouetted against the wider sky. Perhaps it is precisely because of this sense of an open space – an arena inviting display – that a curious phenomenon is to be observed here during the midwinter weeks of Carnival.

In the early morning, the campo is full of people hurrying diagonally across it and disappearing, one way, into the network of *calli* leading towards the Accademia bridge, and the other, over a bridge that leads to the station and Piazzale Roma. There are sharply suited businessmen and businesswomen with briefcases and mobiles; there are parents and children heading for the various schools in the neighbourhood, and students on their way to the university at Cà Foscari. The green-suited street cleaners are brushing rhythmically over the pavements with their old-fashioned brooms, bunches of long twigs bound with string to a knobbly wooden handle.

As the children and I are crossing the *campo*, in the middle of all this bustle there suddenly appears a large and imposing figure. He is dressed from head to foot in the clothes of an eighteenth-century Venetian aristocrat: a skirted, violet satin top coat and violet breeches and an elaborately embroidered apple-green waistcoat. Lace froths at his collar and wrists and his thick cream stockings are fancily gartered with yellow satin. His shoes have handsome brass buckles, two-inch heels and long, squared-tipped toes. In one extravagantly be-ringed hand, he holds a pair of cream leather gloves. He has a wispy little twizzle of a moustache, his powdered cheeks are rouged, and a giant beauty spot is pencilled on to his upper lip.

How tall he really is, I cannot say, but the general impression is of prominence and display. He holds his head high and steps deliberately, ceremoniously across the *campo*, his toes turned out, his silver-topped cane showily extended. He is acutely conscious of whatever impression he thinks he is making on the brisk dog-walkers, the schoolchildren with their rucksacks, and the waitresses having a fag outside the bar. He seems also a little lost – and this not only in time, but also in his own particular fantasy of who he is and where he is. Just peeping over the top of his coat pocket is a German guide book to Venice.

On another morning in the same week, our rush for school is hopelessly slowed by a lady in a vast powdered periwig and a geometrically skirted dress of the seventeenth century. She rustles up the *calle*, brushing both walls with her rectangular skirts, and making it impossible for anybody to squeeze past her. The barrier is in fact a double one, as another lady, similarly skirted, similarly bewigged, paces regally ahead of her. Both women are very fat; their bulging, powdered bosoms, stuck all over with fake beauty spots, are bursting out of a damask corsellage and strings of pearls have been wrapped round and round their fleshy necks. The lady at the front flutters an embroidered fan and chats amiably back over her shoulder to her friend.

I wonder how these people, so consummately and elaborately dressed up, should come to be wandering the streets so very early in the morning? Have they not been to bed at all, but been pacing the city all night long in their finery? Or did they wake hours before dawn and begin the long business of primping and colouring and struggling into corsets? Did they then sally forth into the streets in their splendid bubbles of Venetianness and sail through the commuter crowds, the kids, the students, the twenty-first-century rubbish collectors, blissfully unaware that the year was not in fact 1711, but 2011?

How pleasing that, just for once, it is Venice that provides the workaday backdrop, the banal and the modern, while these petticoated and periwigged visitors, like absurd and over-blown birds of paradise, bring with them, in their overnight bags and their imaginations, some waking dream of a glorious past.

The Venice Effect

HOLLYWOOD HAS, ON various occasions, cast Venice in the unlikely role of a heart-thumping, high-octane action movie location. In the West Coast depictions of this east coast city, speed boats scream up the Grand Canal in a lather of white water, and deep sea divers breathe raspingly through masks as they grapple with gold ingots among the subaqueous foundations of palaces.

The fact of the matter is, of course, that about the most difficult thing to do in Venice is move fast, let alone get away. To every holiday we organize, we must add at least an hour just to get out of the city and join whichever means of land transport we have planned for the next leg of the journey.

Once our suitcases, bags and last-minute bits and pieces have been heaped up on the landing, we have to lug them down four flights of stairs, across the hall and into the *calle*. We then drag and heave them, over uneven pavements, to the *vaporetto* stop where we pile everything into the boat.

This particular section of the journey is a source of squirming embarrassment to me. The mountains of non-Venetian luggage inevitably set off a xenophobic riff from someone in the *vaporetto*. Nothing about us – our language, our clothes, our plastic bags stuffed full of stuff – say anything except Pesky Foreigner, although the more acute observer has, more than once, been visibly intrigued by these tourists who have a large Italian board game sticking out of a box, or a pair of skis, or a bunch of flowers. I tend, pathetically, to speak Italian with the children on these miserable trips and to flaunt my season ticket.

At Piazzale Roma, we must drag and heave everything off again and then, on the pavement, with all our worldly goods spread around us, we wait for the arrival of the green van, which Alberto has gone ahead to fetch from its semi-retirement on a quiet, suburban street in Mestre.

Crime is not a major problem in Venice. Not being able to make a swift getaway from the scene of the crime is a serious deterrent to criminals. When the heist must be followed by a longish walk, a very slow boat ride and a bus journey, the chances of (literally) getting away with it are considerably lowered.

The most successful criminal in Venice will be of the melting-away type, skilled at operating in a crowd; it is rare to go unobserved in this city, even when you think you are alone. This is why there is one particular crime that does flourish here, and within six weeks of my arrival I have fallen victim to it.

It's a Wednesday lunchtime and I'm walking briskly to fetch Freddie from school. I stop briefly at the school door, lean over to kiss him, and we set off for home. It is only during those few seconds of greeting outside the school that anyone could have slipped a hand into my bag and taken my purse. Whoever does it is a pro – not the James Bond sort – but one of the Artful Dodger variety. I feel nothing, and even in those confused first moments of realizing that what should have been there has in fact vanished, I can only admire the slick-fingered technician who has relieved me of forty euros and a sheaf of cards.

Later that afternoon, I return to the school to fetch my other children and I tell some of the waiting parents what has happened. They instantly rally into indignant and purposeful action.

'Gypsies,' says Flavia. 'They send children in squads. They're so small and quick, you notice nothing until you realize that your wallet's gone.'

'They're not interested in the cards,' says Cecilia. 'They throw those away – into the canals or letter boxes. All they want is the cash.'

Another mother, Sara, a quietly spoken and gentle woman, galvanizes into action in that emphatic way that seems to come naturally even to the most pacific Italians.

'Come on!' she says. 'Let's look in the bin.'

She strides across the *calle* towards the rubbish bin.

'Do the rubbish collectors have keys?' I ask in English anguish as she digs her own keys out of her bag and starts to wiggle and manoeuvre one along the edge of the locked front section of the bin. She says nothing, but keeps on fiddling expertly until the lock has been picked and the bin opened. There is no purse inside, but the vigilante parents are still on the case.

'Walk around all the area and look along the ledges on buildings. They quite often dump them up there, once they've taken the cash out.'

'Go to the post office. They've got a room full of wallets that they've found stuffed into letter boxes.'

'My purse was taken once,' Flavia tells me. 'I found it in a boat on the canal. They'd chucked it over the edge. No money in it, of course.'

Grateful and embarrassed in equal measure by the public drama I have triggered, I go, as directed, to report the theft to the police.

The office is in Piazzale Roma and I spend some time walking up and down among buses and taxies before going into a bar for directions. I have already passed the place, but it is poorly marked and fronted with reflecting glass out of which the *carabinieri* can see, without in turn being observed.

I push open the door and enter a very small office. Behind a large desk in the middle of the room, there lounges a policeman in full regalia, down to his elaborate gun holster, peaked, militaristic cap and black shades. He carries on writing for some seconds and, when he finally looks up, does not smile. In fact, he says nothing. He does not offer me a chair, but leaves me to explain, falteringly, apologetically, that I have been robbed. When I have finished, he rises silently to his feet, pushes his chair back with his black-booted heel, and strolls to the iron-grey filing cabinet. That he manages to stroll convincingly across half a metre of space is a tribute to him.

Idly, he leafs through papers. Languidly, he draws one out. He turns, with the elegance of a dancer and the hatchet face of an executioner, to lay the form on the table in front of me. I am mildly panicky and fill it in wrong, but it is clear by now that this is immaterial; we are both engaged in some balletic piece of bureaucracy which will have no outcome and serves no purpose.

The *carabiniere* now returns to his seat. The wide expanse of desk in front of him has nothing on it except for an open packet of Malboro cigarettes. On the otherwise bare walls there is a single large poster showing a black-clad, balaclavaed figure half-crouching and wielding a submachine gun, in an urban landscape of flat rooftops and fire escapes, which has more of downtown Chicago about it than La Serenissima.

I watch the policeman as he signs the documents. He is a strikingly handsome man. If he smiled, he would be all beauty; but smiling is the last thing he has in mind, taken up, as he is, with his dreams, somewhere out there in Malboro Country, Chigaco or the sweating central American jungle, lone ranging it on the *Italian Job* – not tangled up in the Venetian Effect.

Eating Cake

IT IS THE perfect cog in the machinery of the Venetian day – a place to stop, to drink and eat and gossip before carrying on with one's business. It represents the best balance between production and consumption, work and play, nutrition and gastronomy. This is why my favourite *pasticceria* seems to me to be the apex of civilization and why, most days, on my way back from dropping the children at school, I stop off here for a cappuccino and a pastry.

The *pasticceria*, which is a cake shop and café, is small and wood-panelled. The curved bar is a half glassed-in case that is always filled with cakes. In the morning, the central section, under the cash register, is heaped with warm croissants and pastry puffs of pear and chocolate, apple and ricotta, and rich crème patissiere. This is the breakfast section and, if you arrive after ten, you are likely to find it already empty.

The *pasticceria* is run by two energetic and attractive women in their late thirties. They move swiftly and capably about their work, keeping the coffee coming from the silver Gaggia machine; washing cups and glasses; packing cakes to take away in neat parcels, with a knotted ribbon around the paper; chatting with their customers. They are always cheerful; their children drop by on the way home from school; their friends and neighbours go in and out, and at all times of day the *pasticceria* is full of people.

First thing in the morning, the *carabinieri* park their boats outside and saunter in for coffee, laughing and joking in their absurd flak jackets. Passing gondoliers call out for a cold drink, stalling their gondolas by lodging one foot on the wall of the canal, like a bargeman.

'Hey, *bella*, bring me a Coke!'

The young waitress hurries out to hand it over.

When Freddie walks through the door on his way home from school, he gets a similar treatment: the signoras behind the counter take one look and, without so much as asking, they fish his favourite chocolate puff out of the cabinet, wrap it in a paper napkin and hand it over.

As I stand drinking my coffee and greedily savouring every crumb of my pastry, a door in the back of the shop opens and a man in white overalls and a chef's hat comes out carrying a tray of fresh cakes. Behind him, I glimpse the small kitchen, where another baker is rolling out pastry, or piping icing on to biscuits. They are making zabaione puffs, chocolate and chestnut pies, Sicilian cannoli, fruit and custard tartlets, almond slices.

That's when I understand the genius of the *pasticceria* – its perfect, circular logic: the expert industry of two pastry chefs, presented and sold by two amiable and efficient women, bought and consumed by a community of local people for whom the *pasticceria* is breakfast and the proper starting point of every day, or a sandwich at lunchtime, or an aperitif with friends on the way home from work. Two people plus two people plus a community: creative, sociable, local, sustainable, viable – this is good business, this is living well.

Tourists do pass by the *pasticceria*, but it remains, none the less, that rare phenomenon in Venice: a local place. One day, I am there when an Indian couple comes in. The woman has a red bindi painted on her forehead and is wearing a purple silk sari, edged with gold. They order coffee and cakes and are warmly appreciative, marvelling at the decent prices and the excellent pastries. When they have paid for their food, they politely ask the way to San Marco. The Piazza is innumerable twists and turns away from the *pasticceria* and on the other side of the Grand Canal. It is a half-hour walk, if you know the route. For someone living in this quarter of the city it is on the other side of the world. No serious explanation is given to the couple; hands are waved in roughly the right direction and they are told to go straight on, straight on, in the time-honoured Venetian style.

A smart, elderly lady in a fur coat and very red lipstick is standing by the bar and watching all of this. As the door clicks shut behind the couple, she snorts, and remarks tightly to the room in general:

'Hmm! There she was with her third eye and she can't even find her way to San Marco! Ha! These people!'

And everybody in the *pasticceria* laughs – complicit, racist, redneck.

PART 8: March

Bloodlines

The elegant apartments were much appreciated, notably the grand salon Louis XVI, where one admired the head of king Midas, a marvel by Luca della Robbia ... The reception was very lively, and there was a very beautiful musical programme performed by the tziganes. The Princesse Mathilde didn't leave ... until 7 o'clock.

(Paris society newspaper, *Le Gaulois*, 1893)

THE CONTESSA ELENA de Barbarin lives in a palace that bears her name. The land entrance of the Palazzo de Barbarin is an inconspicuous door in a grey stone wall, in a narrow and unremarkable *calle*. The palace's great classical façade can only be approached by water and gives, gloriously, on to the Grand Canal.

The Contessa is a small, vital woman. She inhabits the main floor or *piano nobile* of her family palace, in an unfolding vista of rooms through which she moves with quick energy, her eyes sharp and bright, as though she were one of the Borrowers, come up from under the floorboards to reconnoitre the giant and fantastical world of human beings.

Almost everything in the Contessa's home, other than the Contessa herself, is on the largest of scales. The principal salon is an archipelago

143

of vast and gently moulting gold velvet sofas arranged in clusters among elegant occasional tables of the Louis Quinze variety, a grand piano and the serene lap and spread of Persian carpets. On the walls, dark oil paintings of obscure mythological scenes are borne aloft in frames that are frenzied gilt extravaganzas of leaves and grapes and Roman weaponry.

When the Contessa entertains in these rooms she cuts an elegant, darting figure in her black cocktail dress. Drinks are poured by an ancient servant in an outsized white jacket, with twisted gold brocade epaulettes. The Contessa helps him as he struggles to lift the bottle of prosecco from a silver tray. But despite her gilded life, the Contessa has dreams of elsewhere and they are the perfect inverse of my own, which are mildly envious of such ancient opulence.

On the upper floor, high under the roofs of the Palazzo de Barbarin, Elena has commandeered a room. I say a room, but it is more likely to have been a cupboard in the glory days of the palazzo. It is an average-sized space that would sit quite easily in a far humbler dwelling and, being so high up and therefore not crowded in by other buildings, it is full of light. The walls are painted white and Elena has furnished it simply and sparely – from IKEA.

There is a plain pine table in front of the window, at which she has placed a foldable pine chair. A pine bookcase in a blond-coloured wood stands against one wall and there is a two-seater sofa – square, neat and cream. Beside a glass and steel coffee table, there is a brand-new, pale blue armchair. And that is all: IKEA heaven, nestling in the heart of antiquity.

'Isn't it lovely,' beams the Contessa de Barbarin, sweeping her arm wide in a gesture of triumphant pleasure.

One day in March, Elena de Barbarin calls me with an invitation. A group of Slovak gypsy children are making a day trip to Venice, as part of an Italian tour in which they are performing their traditional singing and dancing. Would we like to come and hear them sing in the *campo* near to where she lives?

Spring has been slow in coming and the city still holds in its bones the damp of a sea-bound winter. We feel the chill in our bodies, too, as we wait for the Rom children to arrive. Elena's talk of a European tour has not prepared me for what I eventually see when they come, tumbling and chattering, into the *campo*. There are about twenty kids, aged from five to seventeen. Raggle-taggle and eager, they quickly draw together, the tallest standing at the back, the little ones at the front, and launch straight into full-throated, hip-swaying song.

They are led by a tall man in late middle age, with a flyaway shock of grey hair and a gaunt, sympathetic face. Smiling delightedly, he accompanies the troupe on his balalaika with frenetic energy; his hand strums the strings so fast, it becomes a blur.

That song is a wild and joyful challenge laid down to winter, to the wealthy, weary, aged city and to all of us, huddled in our monochrome overcoats, on this dreary afternoon.

First, the girls step forward. They begin, slowly, to weave around each other, twisting their wrists with the languid elegance of Indian dancers, then rotating their hips like belly-dancers before shaking and shimmying their shoulders and limboing precipitously backwards, their long, shining black hair dipping to the pavement behind.

Next come the boys, springing forward like a band of juvenile Cossacks, knees bent, side-kicking out, arms folded rigid in front. They straighten up and begin a kind of frenzied tap dance, whacking out the staccato rhythm on their own bodies – flat hands on thighs, arms, chests: a drum roll of the flesh.

Alongside the bigger boys, three miniature tikes hip-hop the same manic tattoo. The smallest of them cannot be more than five years old. He has a snubby, merry, knowing face; his thatch of black hair is dyed a strangely flat orange colour; he is wearing a faded Hawaiian shirt, worn-out jeans and no socks, and a pair of ancient, flaking gym shoes. He seems half animated puppet, half child.

Two of the older boys now step up and lift him on to their shoulders. The tiny boy surveys the crowd that has gathered to watch him. Then, every muscle in his body rises to the occasion as he opens his wide mouth and lets out a sinuous, minor-key wail so holleringly loud that the vein in his scrawny neck swells and pulses.

Up there on his shoulder-top eyrie, he throws his arms wide and, with consummate showmanship, holds the note for what feels like several long minutes. It is a defiant, bellowing lament of such world-weary pain that it does not seem possible from an infant's mouth.

But the fact is, of course, that we are not simply watching as one small boy sings. In that comic Pinocchio, in those drawn-out moments, there inhere generations of shared knowledge and shared experience. His actual age is spectacularly irrelevant, because this child of a rootless people embodies a longer and more unbroken lineage of experience than I myself (old enough to be his grandmother) could dream of.

These Rom children, whose language uses the same word to express both 'yesterday' and 'tomorrow' have a grip on time, a foothold in it, born of a social unity, and through that a historical continuity, of which I have no notion, to which I can only bear astonished witness.

My own ragged family tree more or less disappears from sight in different places in the nineteenth century – some of my ancestors came from Scotland, some from Denmark and Hungary, some from England. The odd, mythical drift leads further back, to a medieval Cornish church register; to France, through the resonance of a beautiful Huguenot name; then further afield again, to the rumoured wreck of a Portuguese galleon off the coast of fifteenth-century Jamaica and the subsequent settlement in Kingston of a community of Sephardic Jews. These threads are mere secondhand stories for me, pretty fragments of exotica.

As we sit watching the gypsy children singing and dancing, my friend Enrico leans over and nods at Elena and the Rom.

'You'll never in your life have been in the presence of two such different groups of people,' he says quietly.

But later, it occurs to me that, in a certain way, this is not right. What Elena de Barbarin and the Rom children have in common, what has been denied to me, is a powerful sense of who they are that is rooted in their clan, their lineage, their bloodline. My own feeble gleanings of emigrations and the exigencies of an empire that cast its people all around the earth, until they became, in name at least, citizens of other cultures, leave me, not Elena, not the gypsy children, without a home, without a name or ancient family.

Commuters

ARTURO MARCON IS small, but perfectly formed – a wiry, muscular man, with a square face, white hair and a brisk, grey moustache. His large, black-framed spectacles give even more weight to his commanding head. Arturo is sixty-nine years old and walks with the confident strut of a general. His wife Lucia is shorter still and considerably wider. Her thin hair is dyed a surprising, dense red that has no equivalent in nature; her lost eyebrows have been forcefully redefined; her skin, tanned over decades of sea wind and beach sun, is heavily wrinkled. She is a year younger than her husband, though she looks fifteen years older. In this, they are a typical Venetian couple of the older generation: the man, limber-fit after a lifetime of rowing, of jumping on and off boats, of manhandling cargo; the woman, spreading widely sideways, despite her decades of cleaning and cooking, and now waddling, comfortably, to a standstill.

Their family is Venetian from as far back as anyone knows. Lucia, gossiping with me one day, stops abruptly in mid-sentence:

'Madonna! I find it hard not to speak dialect when I'm talking like this!'

What she means is that gossip is intimate talk; friends gossip and it requires a degree of trust. One's own argot is the natural place for that kind of confidence, and while to Lucia the Italian language is public, official and formal, Venetian is private and personal and expresses who she really is and what she wants to say. All of this I understand very well, spending my days as I do, attempting to be myself in a language that is not my own.

In the streets of Venice there are many people like the Marcons. If you look, you will see them. They often share the same melancholy secret: at the end of the day, these Venetians button up their jackets, shoulder their bags, and head for the bus station at Piazzale Roma. These Venetians sleep elsewhere.

Arturo and Lucia live in an apartment in a modern block in Marghera, on the mainland. Every morning they get up, dress, drink their coffee and leave the house. They walk down the street to the bus stop through a landscape of 1970s developments. The traffic at this time – half-past seven – is heavy on the busy main road. They wait patiently at the bus stop, like all the other workers, except that they are ten years past retirement age and have a different, rugged, homely look, more fisherman than commuter. But commuters they are. Arturo and Lucia commute daily to their home. They, like many Venetians, have been denied a basic right – to lay their heads down in their own home – by the greed of landlords, hungry for the tourist rentals that bring in much higher rates than residential lets, and the vertiginous ascent of real estate prices.

Ask them, and they will tell you that they dream of living their last years back home. Not on this *terraferma*, among the *forestieri* – the forest dwellers, the landlubbers – but out there, in their city on water. Venice is their village, their place.

Arturo and Lucia left twenty years ago when yet another disastrous high water flooded their apartment.

'I couldn't take it any more,' Arturo tells me. 'I said to Lucia: "That's enough! We're leaving. We'll get a well-built, dry new house on *terraferma*." '

The bus moves quickly across the causeway which links Venice to the mainland. Arturo, through his huge spectacles, follows the progress of a lone rower, moving in his *sandolo* across to Campalto. He knows the boy; it's Andrea Zen, Franco's grandson. He's training for the regatta next weekend. He needs to improve that grip if he wants to have a chance of winning.

The bus passes the petrol station and slows into the one-way system of Piazzale Roma. It comes to a standstill among the ranks of other buses, and the office workers, the tourism servicers, the cleaners, the trinket-sellers, the waiters all pile out and Lucia and Arturo step down too. The Marcons' job is, after all, perhaps more specialized than Venice. Their job is being Venetian.

Together, they walk eastward. Lucia will spend the morning

cooking and cleaning for her brother who lives alone near the Arsenale. Arturo will go to the boat club, where he is a stalwart and elder, and coaches the younger members in their rowing skills. When he is not out in a boat, he sits on the waterfront with the other members, surveying the great, glittering panorama of his city, and arguing about who should be the next club president.

Like all ageing migrants, these displaced Venetians yearn for home and gather in their little ghettos. But uniquely, perhaps, they have been forced into a sort of halfway existence in which they partake of, but do not fully possess, their city. Were they not so solid, you might think that they are ghosts. Like ghosts, they walk down the narrow streets, between the chic and gleaming art galleries, where there were once (not long ago – five, ten years) butchers and bakers, a dairy, a greengrocer. They have, in a way, been condemned to the status of tourist in their own city. It is hard to imagine how foreign these shiny, modern outlets must seem, how very far from home.

On the sad days, the whole of Venice might appear to them to be some kind of exquisite Purgatory – an in-between world where no one fully exists, neither the drifting, gobbling tourists, nor the Venetians themselves.

Kites

CAMPO DEL GHETTO, the centre of the Jewish quarter, has a constant military presence. A small hut appears to have been plumped down on the paving stones and is often occupied by a couple of grey-uniformed soldiers. I do not understand what they are doing there.

On a windy spring afternoon I go to sit in the *campo*, on a bench, in the sunshine. The blue sky is hectic with dashes of white cloud; it is a day for high spirits and children are racing around the open space, shrieking.

Over to one side is a small group of young men flying kites, basic structures made of two bamboo sticks bound together in a cross and covered with a diamond of white tissue paper. The men are flying them expertly, on the ends of long strings, and managing, for the most part, to avoid the branches of the great plane trees that grow in the *campo*.

Adults and children have gathered around the kite-flyers, heads back, necks arched, marvelling at the neat aerobatics and feeling themselves airborne and flying up there too in that bright spring sky. Everything is simple and good.

Then the door of the hut opens and two soldiers saunter out. They are both in full uniform, one elongated and weasely, the other (coming up no higher than his colleague's shoulder) square and porcine. Their skin is pallid and their heads close shaven under those caps. They stroll indolently towards the kite-flyers, gun holsters bumping on their hips, relishing the *High Noon* approach and the gratifying prospect of wielding power.

The kite-flyers, by comparison, are wind and water – small, slim men, dark-skinned, with long black hair streaming as they run, offering up their treasures to the sky. They come, perhaps, from Syria or Iran, or further east again.

When the soldiers arrive, the diamond kites slide down from the sky, like charmed snakes. They lie inert on the stones of the Ghetto. I watch as documents are taken from coat pockets. I see the slow flick through pages; the weighty look at photo, then man, then photo again; the peering at names and other foreign data that are meaningless except for their being foreign. It takes a while. At a certain point, it must dawn on the two soldiers that there is nothing whatsoever amiss. The time for retrieving their dignity is suddenly tight, so they thumb some more and look and compare some more, until it is unavoidably up. Then they hand back the documents, turn on their booted heels, and retreat to their hutch.

The children and happy parents gather again, the kite-flyers offer up their dancing kites once more, and for another little while, life is good in the Campo del Ghetto.

PART 9: April

Crabs

THERE IS A constant flow of people in and out of Venice; there are many beachings and innumerable brief landings and sometimes the strangest combinations of individuals wash up together on these island shores.

One sunny afternoon in April, Roland has two friends over to play after school. Apart from the fact that they are all nine years old, these three children have very little in common. Bai is a sturdy boy who has recently arrived in Venice with his mother from one of the easternmost points of the ex-Soviet empire – Kyrgyzstan. He has almond Asiatic eyes, a perfectly round, coffee-coloured face and a thick, black, shiny fringe. He is strong and smiling and talks with the plaintive lilt of a native Russian speaker. When I first met cheerful Bai, I could not have guessed at his troubled story. His mother's face, her forehead creased into lines of deep anxiety, of grief even, was a bleak testimony to what had brought them to Venice. She and her husband had decided that they could no longer raise a child in their violent and troubled homeland.

'I couldn't even play in the square outside my house,' Bai tells us cheerily, over lunch. 'There were too many guns. They were always shooting people in my street. My friend was shot.'

So Bai's mother has brought her youngest son to Venice, while her husband stays on in Kyrgyzstan, with the intention of joining them as soon as he can find work.

Her grown-up daughter has left too, and gone to live in Turkey with her husband and baby. Bai's is a family scattered by violent civil unrest to different corners of Europe. Now, his mother works as a house-keeper and companion to a rich old Venetian woman. Bai has to stay away from the house for as long as possible every day, out from under his mother's feet and away from her employer's ear shot. This is why he is often at our house.

Our other guest is Dea. She too has recently arrived in the city. Her father, an Italian-American writer, famous for various high-profile Hollywood screenplays, has decided to bring his family to Europe for a year while he works on his next film. They have rented a floor of a palazzo on the Grand Canal (practically next door to Bai's mother's employer). Dea, Roland and Bai are in the same class at school. Dea is wilful and feisty and funny. Roland, Dea and Bai are, all three, forces to be reckoned with. This, after all, is what they really have in common.

'We're going to catch crabs,' they announce, after lunch.

There is a great, teeming life of crabs in the canal near to our house. The smallest can be 2 centimetres across, the largest might reach a width of 10 centimetres. They scuttle and bounce up and down the stone walls, among shifting fronds of pale green weed, like miniature aquatic absailers. Roland's stories of derring-do at this time mostly revolve around how many tens of these hapless creatures he has managed to scoop up in an afternoon and he, Dea and Bai are well-armed for the hunt, with nets and plastic boxes.

The crabs are, in fact, edible and, in the right season, when their shells are soft, are prized as a local delicacy, *moeche*. They are caught and then left to scramble about for a couple of days in a tub filled with milk, which they thoroughly absorb into their bodies. When they are finally deep fried and eaten whole, they are a rich dish. Today, the kids just throw them back in the canal.

Although Bai and Roland are old hands at crabbing, it occurs to me that Dea is new to the game so I should, at least for the first time, go down to the canal with them and keep an eye on the proceedings. I roll up my newspaper, push my reading glasses up onto my head, and wander after them, with the intention of leaning against a wall in the sunshine and catching up on the news while they fish.

But as we reach the water's edge, it comes to me in a flash that this is, quite simply, impossible. I must follow the crab fishing with unswerving attention; the newspaper must remain rolled; the reading glasses perched on top of my head. Why? Certainly not for fear that my beloved son might come to harm in the torpid waters of the Venetian Lagoon; neither am I worried for the little Kyrgyz boy, whose mother has left home and husband to bring him to safety in a foreign land. No, the phantom that so suddenly, so violently, rears its head is the terrifying apparition of the massed forces of the Hollywood legal system.

Thirteen years into chaotic motherhood and four children down the line, and I have never before this moment gone into a sweat of anxiety about any child's health and safety. Not even a light perspiration. Now, I am darting up and down the waterfront inches behind the oblivious Dea as she leans vertiginously, perilously over the edge to scoop up crabs.

'There's one!' she shouts to the boys, then darts suddenly to right or to left, as sideways scuttling as any of her quarry. And I, hovering at her side, am plucking pathetically at her silky fur gilet and whispering desperately in her heedless ear, 'Careful, Dea! Not too far, Dea! Oooh – no, Dea, you're too close to the edge!'

A simple fall in the water, I calculate, followed by a bedraggled fishing out (sodden gilet, howling princess), would be headline stuff, possibly even a court summons. A blow to the body on stone or boat would, unquestionably, bring life imprisonment. Concussion ... broken limbs ... brain damage – extradition, Death Row, lethal injection. And as I dart and clutch and implore, the tourists pass by, wandering happily, post-prandially, towards the famous art collection nearby.

Many of them stop, and there are multi-tongued exclamations of delight at the charming sight of two small boys and a girl scooping up crabs and depositing them in Tupperware. The crabbing has created an international waterside traffic jam, a Babel of sentimentality and click-ing cameras.

How blissfully unaware they are, these holidaymakers, of the mind-boggling complexities of geopolitics, of class, of vicissitude and privilege embodied in these three kids who are innocently fishing in the most beautiful city in the world, on a warm April afternoon. And as for me, it is at this point that I see how, despite my best liberal instincts, my worthiest anthropologizings, I – running scared before a vision of the law – have a great deal more in common with the franti-cally scuttling crabs, side-slipping and intent on escape, than with any of the human beings present here.

That is, I suppose, when my spectacles slip off my head and sink gently into the dim silt of the canal and I shriek:

'OK! That's it! We're going home!'

Cassandra

IN THE NEXT *calle* to us there lives a very old woman. Her mumbly old chin bristles with the beginnings of a beard and age has left her sexless, formless: a bag-of-potatoes, cartoon granny, bundled up in a shabby man's overcoat. She is the Cassandra of Dorsoduro: its ranting, warning prophetess.

In the morning, she positions herself against railings at the point where a busy thoroughfare opens into a small *campo*. She leans heavily on the handle of her shopping trolley, glaring through heavy-rimmed glasses at the passers-by – enemies and allies alike. Stapled to the front of her trolley is a large sheet of paper, covered in thick, black capital letters – an obsessively insistent calligraphy which fifty per cent of the people who pass her could not read. They are the enemy.

'VENEZIA – HAS BECOME A HOTEL – WE VENETIANS ARE LIKE THE PIGEONS – A RACE OF LOSERS – TO BE EXTERMINATED – VENEZIA IS NO LONGER THE HOME OF THE VENETIANS – BUT ONE ENORMOUS B&B – '

... and so on, each half-literate dash a crie de coeur, unnoticed by the crowds that flood past, babbling in every language under the sun but Cassandra's.

Cassandra: ancient, furious, impotent, mad, right – and the happy, oblivious faces of holidaymakers who, if they notice anything at all, see a funny old bag lady – a woman who feeds the stray cats perhaps? – a comic aberration among smooth marble, witty ironwork and the languid lap of water.

Hey, You!

THERE IS ONE small Italian word that triggers deep anxiety in me. It is a word that forcefully reminds me of my alien status in this country because it carries on its narrow shoulders a whole system of behaviour, an entire social order that I do not fully understand. Understand, that is, in the way I understand my mother tongue – the way I live its glancing ironies, its quirks and trip-wires, its serendipities and its assumptions about who is what and where: the complete world it gives to me.

This troublesome little word is 'tu' and its accomplice – the only slightly larger 'lei'. They are, respectively, the informal and formal second person singular for which the English language now has only one word: 'you'.

'Tu' and 'lei' belong to a linguistic system in which social difference is both negotiated and declared in public. To a Briton, and I suspect to other English speakers such as Americans and Australians, this is an awkward business, revealing as it does anxieties and hypocrisies about our societies that we might prefer not to confront.

I first begin to understand something of this while I wait for my children in the cavernous and unlovely *calle* outside the elementary school. Here, I sometimes chat with a girl who works as an au pair for one of the other mothers. Her name is Barbara. She comes from a small Veneto town, about an hour away by train. She is in her early twenties and is studying Italian literature at the University of Venice.

She is a pleasant, friendly young woman.

After several weeks during which she addresses me with the formal 'lei', I say to her, one day, casually, taking it as a given: 'Let's use "tu".'

I know that as the older person, it is for me to make this move and I assume that this is all that is needed to put things between us on a less formal linguistic footing. To my surprise she looks stricken.

'Oh no,' she says. 'I couldn't.'

I persist, still not fully understanding.

'You know it really doesn't mean anything to us English. We don't use these different forms and it doesn't come naturally to me.'

But, of course, the opposite doesn't come naturally to Barbara either: the linguistic shift that would allow me to relax would make her profoundly uncomfortable. Indeed, it is clear from her reaction that she is almost physically incapable of getting her tongue around the words when speaking to me. Of course, I give in – what else can I do? – and we settle with an even more awkward situation in which I address her as 'tu' and she continues to use 'lei' for me.

But what is this discomfort of mine? Why should this little word have such power?

What makes me squirm, I begin to think, is that I hear the lei/tu distinction as an overt statement of hierarchy – of my elevated status in relation to Barbara.

A significant amount of our collective social energy in Britain is taken up with trying to hide, deny even, the class divisions that rend our society like ancient, but still active, fault lines. I remember my grandmother, Pamela. Born in 1913, she was the only child of a British Raj engineer, a tall, handsome man named Reginald, with handlebar moustaches and a stiff white collar. I have a picture of Reginald and my great-grandmother Olive on their wedding day, in Southsea, in 1908. It is a group photograph, complete with bridesmaids, matrons of honour, best man and assorted relations, and is a magnificent, Edwardian extravaganza of white lace, big hats, bursting bouquets. This is upper-middle-class Imperial Britain in its last throes, but displayed at its finest.

Despite being born into this world, my grandmother had an

instinctively egalitarian temperament. She rejected the forms and strictures of her Victorian parents and became a painter of bohemian leanings, who interested herself in people for their own sakes and was warmly responsive to their personal qualities, and yet, whenever she spoke about someone, almost the first piece of information to come out of her mouth was where he or she stood in the byzantine structures of the early twentieth-century British social order into which, willy-nilly, she had been born.

Mr Briggs, she might have said, was a lovely man: lower middle class, a sensitive gardener, the best of neighbours, and a talented amateur painter. She was blithely unconscious of the acute inner pressure to say not only what kind of a person Mr Briggs was, but also where he stood on the scaffolding of society and therefore, by extension, where he stood in relation to her.

In modern Britain, this story is not over: up and down the land, these hierarchies, shored up by a divided and divisive education system and by the subtleties of accent and idiom, are in places as ingrained as they were one hundred years ago. They are imprinted on our collective consciousness like photographic negatives; they are part of the DNA of our culture. We operate by them, we are intensely aware of them, but most of the time we do not dare to speak their name.

It is from this world shot through with the denial of social distinctions that I come. But now, I find myself in Italy, where the informal and formal second person singular leave no one in any doubt about their relation to the person with whom they are talking – and it makes me nervous. None of the fake chumminess of the universal 'you' here; no brushing under the carpet of social forms: it is all out there in that one little word.

But that is the real question: what exactly *is* all out there?

It is true, of course, that all human beings recognize and express status of one kind or another, but even having acknowledged this the British class system ranks right up there for its elaborate, ingrained and divisive hierarchy. Italy, of course, has its aristocracy and its vast discrepancies of wealth, and all the distinctions these create, but despite that it seems to me a more egalitarian society. It differs from

Britain in two critical ways: first, that there is no significant private school sector and, second, that an individual's accent does not tell you what social class they belong to, but quite simply from which part of the peninsula they come. The 'tu' and the 'lei' do not, therefore, reveal hidden divisions in the society; what they usually signify is something simpler: degrees of familiarity and formality.

Barbara, the student au pair, addresses me formally because I am twenty years her senior. This is an unavoidable fact, a neutral fact – an accident of history – and is to nobody's discredit. She, as a young woman, is merely according me the respect I deserve as an older woman. I have lived longer than she has and am the mother of several children. I bear more responsibility and therefore have more authority and deserve more respect.

It strikes me as a decent enough social equation. Every one of us, after all, must pass through the same hoops; each of us is born, grows up, takes on responsibilities, gains experience and accrues, in the process, the right to be respected, a right that is then formally enshrined in the building blocks of the language – its grammar. It's hardly a democratic right, but there's a kind of fairness in it: you earn your colours by living and getting older. What is being expressed here is not class distinction, but social difference. So what's my problem?

There is a profound, perhaps even pernicious, error common in the Anglo-Saxon-based, English-speaking cultures. This is the idea that informality is equivalent to equality; that anything casual and apparently unstructured is somehow inherently democratic. So, there is the illusion that the laddish or charming or earnest politician, say, is just like any other bloke on the street, while the plain fact remains that anyone that hungry for power and attention is, to put it politely, a breed apart. As David Cameron jokes in an open-necked polo shirt in Cornwall, Afghanistan of course continues to burn. In Italy, they know that all of this boy-next-door stuff is dangerous nonsense. That is why Berlusconi's tours around the peninsula on his luxury yacht were an intrinsic part of his electioneering and of his popular appeal. While this may not be preferable, it is at least an unashamed acknowledgement that although he undoubtedly wished to be the People's Man,

Berlusconi was definitely not a Man of the People.

And, of course, I cannot pretend to be Barbara's equal, or not, that is, in the sense of being the same as her. Which brings me face to face with what I suspect is the deeper reason for my feelings of awkwardness when she refuses to recognize me linguistically as her peer.

As I chat with this young woman, twenty years my junior, I do so under the illusion that I am hardly much older than her. So that when I invite her to address me as 'tu' I assume that it would seem as natural to her as it does to me. It doesn't. Barbara, who is not in my head, sees me for exactly what I am: a middle-aged mother of four, old enough to be her mother. She has no difficulty with the fact that we are neither contemporaries, nor friends. What I take for her friendliness is, in fact, politeness: basic, decent, irreproachable good manners. Barbara forces me to slough off the pitiful illusion that I am Forever A Girl.

So the Italian 'tu' and the 'lei' work together to correct the dual fantasy of equality and immortality. Brilliant. But I keep on getting them wrong; they are still not properly lodged under my skin. In the middle of a spectacular row, in Italian, with Alberto, I become so incensed, so enraged, that there are no words for my spluttering anger. So how, my Anglo-logic reasons, inflamed with fury, can I possibly address this vile man in the intimate 'tu' form? I understand 'tu' as soft and friendly; clearly 'lei', the formal 'you', is the only way to speak to someone you hate. I launch into the 'lei'. It backfires. For some seconds he is bemused, then he begins to laugh.

'What are you talking about?' he asks.

I'm not sure, but it feels, obscurely, right. My wrathful logic strikes Alberto, however, as hysterically funny; it is a kind of personal and linguistic gobbledegook. The argument fizzles out.

Later, I try to understand how my use of 'lei' must have sounded to this native Italian speaker. I imagine a British couple in the middle of a violent row. Suddenly the woman who is screaming at her husband 'You fucking bastard!', morphs, without warning, into a character in a Jane Austen novel and starts addressing him instead, with froideur, with hauteur, as 'Mr Bennett'.

It would, I can see, be hard to keep a straight face.

Real Estate Heaven

WHEN PIETRO CASOLA announced, in 1495, that everything there was to say about Venice had already been said, he slipped on the banana skin of history. His mistake – a common one – was radically to under-estimate both the dead and those not yet born. That is how he became a dupe of modernity.

'Because I am alive and conscious now,' this logic seems to go, 'the reality to which I am witness must be the definitive one.'

This is the logic of children (when I am not there, nothing is there) and of infantile despots: 'Before me: nothing.'

Casola was a man of the Renaissance, the breeding ground of the modern world. All around him thinkers and artists were re-defining and re-expressing the world in terms of their own individual and human consciousness. What happened subsequently in European history could not have occurred without this first, critical shift in point of view. When Michelangelo sculpted God in the shape of a perfect man, did he have any idea that his act of exquisite devotion was part of a fundamental undermining of God's hegemony in Western civilization?

God and the gods offered us heaven, reminded us of Arcadia, but once human beings took the helm it followed that we had also taken into our own hands the possibility of perfection; we could (at least) aspire to the creation of perfection: heaven on earth, and once that was possible a whole new raft of problems started to shift and blunder downstream and the twentieth century cut its devastating swathe through history as the century of hellish Utopias.

Not every culture in the world has sloughed off history with as much alacrity as our own. What modernized Europe came to perceive as the chains of the past, others continued to value as roots, and inte-gral to their living identity.

In spring, my friend Gloria comes to visit me in Venice. Gloria is Bolivian; on her mother's side, she is Spanish in origin; on her father's side, she is Aymara Indian. She has the oval face, long straight nose and almond eyes of an indigenous Andean.

One morning, I take Gloria to visit one of my favourite Venetian palazzi, an ancient building, heavy with the odour of the past, in which even the walls reveal the strata of centuries of change: fragments of fresco, stripped back to plaster, to brick, to wood.

Slowly, we walk together from hall to silent hall, savouring the shadowy tapestries and unfolding spaces until we finally emerge into daylight and on to the *loggia* or terrace. The great trunk of wisteria that twists up the front of the building showers the *loggia* with a cool, violet explosion of flowers. The courtyard below is full of April sunshine, warming the stone pavement. Gloria and I sit down on a bench, in the shade of the wisteria, and breathe in its sweet and heavy scent.

'I would love to live here,' I say.

Gloria shudders and shakes her head.

'I wouldn't. There have been too many lives here. Think of all those people! Century after century, living and suffering here.'

All swept up in my lazy, hedonistic dream of a Real Estate Heaven (you can get anything you desire, if you just have the money), I have seen in the palazzo, merely, a gorgeous thing that I wish to possess. What Gloria sees are other people's real lives stretching back from where she happens to be standing in time. She feels the ghosts of them crowding in, hears them telling their stories – their true stories. Her sense of herself, her aesthetic, her emotions are bound up not only with what is happening to her now, but also with what has come before her. Her sense of history is of an unfolding story in which she and all of humanity are active participants. Her relationship to the world around her comes from an understanding of time that is fundamentally differ-ent from mine. To Gloria, the dead are her parents, the unborn – her children. I, by contrast and entirely unconsciously, see myself, as had Casola, riding the crest of Time's Wave. Had I been alive eighty years ago, I might have expressed this childlike belief in modernity in the conviction that I could help to create a brave new world. I might, like my liberal, optimistic, perhaps naive grandparents in the 1930s, have joined the Communists. Now, in 2009, all of that has soured: the twen-tieth century saw the tragic corruption of high ideals into murderous ideologies; now, we are witness to a meltdown into decadence: Utopian idealism has been appropriated by consumerism. We no longer aspire to creating heaven on earth; we now believe that we can buy it.

And so back to Venice, where the living city continues to fight an ever-weakening rearguard action and its stones are sold to tourists for a long weekend of Mini Break Heaven.

PART 10: May

Other Lives

WHEN MARY JANE comes to visit, she draws my attention to something I have not noticed before about the tourists in Venice.

'It's white tourism,' she says. 'You hardly see any black people here.'

She is right. The same is true of the inhabitants, which strikes me as strange really, in a city that must once have been a racial and cultural melting pot on the scale of contemporary New York or London. Just look at the paintings of 400 to 500 years ago, where turbaned Turks and Moorish merchants and sailors and servants rub shoulders with the native Venetians.

In one of Carpaccio's great, thronging scenes of fifteenth-century Venetian life, a black gondolier leans against his oar. He was probably a slave. And then, of course, there is one of the most famous – if fictional – Venetians of them all: Shakespeare's Othello, who was no slave, but a general in the Venetian army.

Nowadays, virtually the only people of African origin on the streets of Venice are the so-called Vu-compra – the illegally employed, often Somali, vendors of fake designer bags and sunglasses, who wander in small groups, strikingly visible with their shining black skin and great height, head and shoulders above the crowds, lugging their bundles of contraband goods and speaking in bubbling, rounded vowels that are unintelligible to most of the people around them.

One evening I am at a talk in Ca' Rezzonico, one of the great Venetian palazzos and now its museum of the eighteenth century. Recently restored, it is a gleaming monument to power and money; the vast salons are decorated with trompe l'oeuil marble columns, mythological scenes, gods and maidens looking down from vertiginous balconies, painted statues breaking into monochrome life.

The talk is taking place in the ballroom and the lecturer's voice ricochets off the marble floors and stuccoed walls so that I, with my foreigner's ear, fail to catch half of what he is saying. Eventually, I give up straining to hear and pass the hour studying the absurdly grandiloquent space around me. This is when I notice the black men. They are placed at intervals around the ballroom. They are about a metre high and carved from ebony. With one hand, they raise aloft a sort of tray, suitable, perhaps, for a single vase. Their bodies are perfectly athletic and artfully displayed, a hand on a hip, one knee slightly bent, the magnificent gleaming torso turned so as to reveal the musculature at its very best. It is an alluring, slightly feminine pose, but what it showcases is pure masculinity. Up to this point, one might describe them as having a certain erotic camp. But these statues are not eighteenth-century erotica, they are eighteenth-century pornography. What makes the difference? The shocking addition of perfectly carved wooden chains that hang around their necks and down to a shackle on their wrists.

As I look at them, I wonder about the kind of guests the family Rezzonico would have entertained in this salon in its heyday. There were unlikely to have been many Africans, but surely, every so often, there would have been a Moorish ambassador or merchant – or general – present. What would they have made of these fashionable, lascivious images of black flesh displayed around the hall? Would these carved slaves have been considered offensive? Of course not. An image of this kind would have had little or no impact on any black grandee strolling through the state rooms of this palazzo in his finery. Just as the carvings inhabit a limited aesthetic space somewhere between grotesquerie, pornography and erotica, so the subjects of the carvings – black slaves – would have been outside the consciousness of the rich and noble who looked at them, and this separation had little to do with the colour of their skin. All that counted here was the absence of freedom and status, not as individuals, but as chattels.

None of this is news: shared skin colour never was a guarantee of fellow feeling or proof of common experience. I think of my own inability to connect with or understand the gypsy beggars. I think of other much, much worse crimes.

Mary Jane is right; the vast majority of people in this once richly cosmopolitan city are white skinned and of European descent. This means that Venice is not, at this point in its history, truly a metropolis. Now, in the early twenty-first century a city is, by its very nature, multi-ethnic, socially multifaceted. This is no longer Venice's story. The city has become a village resort, to which the wealthy of the world flock for their pleasure.

A significant proportion of the cosmopolitan life that still survives here is essentially unintegrated, culturally and politically; it is to be found among the immigrants, legal and illegal, who serve and service the city and who live either outside or below the resident social classes. There are, on the streets of Venice, people who come not just from other places, but from other worlds – and they are here not for pleasure, but through tough necessity. Most of them cannot afford the rents in the city and migrate every night to Mestre or Marghera to sleep under cheaper roofs.

Unlikely though it may at first seem, Venice is still a frontier town: a possible first port of call for people entering the European Union, often illicitly. I know people from Romania, Moldova, Kyrgyzistan and they are not tourists. These are some of their stories.

The Weather in Moldova

WE DECIDE, IN January, to postpone the twins' birthday party until the warm weather comes and we can hold it outside, in the park. Which is why, having waited so long, when the May day arrives and it is dull and drizzly, I am determined not to cancel. That – and the fact that I am

English, not Italian, and think a little rain never hurt anyone. Besides which, I have cooked the pizzas and made a cake in the shape of a pirate's chest, stuffed with chocolate coins and now leering bulbously in several directions.

The phone calls begin early in the day, at least five hours before the party is due to start.

'Hello, this is Paola, Fosca's mother. Is the party still on, with the weather like this?'

'Oh yes. Obviously if it's raining ...'

'Oh, yes, obviously. OK then, let's hope it clears up.'

Just about every mother in the class rings at some point during the decidedly variable afternoon, but I remain cheerfully, resolutely, stubbornly Anglo-Saxon about the weather and the importance of sticking to our plans.

So, at three o'clock, we set off for the park. I carry the unsteady pirate's chest and Lily drags a shopping trolley full of drinks and cups and plates and Tupperware boxes. She is also trailing a large bunch of bright balloons that seem, on that grey, deserted waterfront, only to advertise our folly.

As we make a slow progress over the bridges, my mobile rings. It's Paola again.

'I'm so sorry, but with this weather, I'm afraid Fosca won't be able to come to the party.'

We labour on. When we arrive at the park, it is empty. The rain, which is coming down quite hard now, is dripping from the dark trees; the balding grass is dissolving into mud patches. We choose a spot under an umbrella pine, next to a low wall, on top of which we spread floral paper cloths and lay out the pizza, crisps, cupcakes and, of course, the treasure chest. Then we rig up balloons on the pieces of broken neo-classical statuary that lie around our chosen picnic spot. We have, I think proudly, stepping back to survey things, made a good job of it: there is a cheerful, making-do-in-spite-of-the-odds look to it: an eccentric little bower of English partyishness in this gloomy afternoon park. Cath Kidston would be proud of us.

At a quarter-past four, the sun, as if taking pity on us, comes out.

In a beautiful clean sweep, the dank little park is transformed into a sparkling place: the sky is washed clean, the air warm again. This is Italy of course and May has only been temporarily eclipsed. As if by sympathetic magic, and only one hour late, a band of children races through the gates, carrying presents and ready for action.

'Oh, the rain!' smiles one of the mothers, when I apologize, as though personally responsible for the weather. 'Nothing would have stopped us from coming!'

I could kiss the woman.

So the children play among the trees, and the flotsam and jetsam of renaissance masonry and we, the mothers, sit chatting and eating cake in the sharply lovely late afternoon sunshine.

After a while, I notice that a young woman is sitting slightly apart from the others. I know that she is nanny to one of the children. We have talked a couple of times, making arrangements for playing or picking up children; she is from Moldova. I move over to sit with her.

She is an attractive, high-cheekboned woman in her late twenties; her expression is severe and closed.

'How do you like living in Venice?' I ask her.

'It's OK,' she says, unsmiling. 'But I miss my children.'

'You have children? How old are they?' I don't mean to sound surprised.

'They are nine and four. I haven't seen them for a year.'

'Why so long?'

'I need 2,000 euros in my bank account so that I can get into Italy to work. Even if I just go back to Moldova for a holiday, I must show the Italian authorities I still have the money in my account. I can't afford to do that. I have to send all the money back to my husband, for the family.'

I have only a sketchy idea of where Moldova is.

'So wages are higher in Italy than in Moldova?' I ask.

'Yes. No one who works in Moldova can afford the cost of living there. What I earn in one week here, I would earn in one month at home. The shops in Moldova base their prices on what foreign workers send back. It has become impossible to live in Moldova and work there.'

167

She never once smiles, but she talks freely, in this sun-filled park, bouncing with happy kids, none of them hers. She is a mother forced, not only to live apart from her children, but, in a vile twist of economic irony, to endure the spectacle of other, united mothers and children, and to be, herself, the carer of another woman's son.

Katerina's Story

WHEN KATERINA COMES to clean, I like her immediately. She is small and wiry, with high cheekbones, black eyes and straight black hair. She has a humorous, indignant manner and is visibly a woman of extremes. She is tough and generous and bossy. On the first morning, she tells me her story:

'Eight years ago, I needed to get work. I couldn't afford to live in Moldova any more. I paid 1,200 euros to some smugglers to get me into Italy. The journey took three weeks. There were ten people in my group and a guide. We travelled with our rucksacks on our backs, that was all.

'They put us in coaches and took us to the Austrian border. Then we had to walk through Austria. Mostly, we went through the forests, to avoid being seen. We would walk all day, and at night we would stop and the guide would dig up food and bedding that had been left buried in the earth or in piles of leaves by the last group to pass through. I was so tired, I would not lie down to sleep because I was afraid that I would never get up again.

'Sometimes, the border guards shot at us, or pretended to, trying to scare us. We would panic and run. I hurt my foot running.

'I can never look at sweetcorn now. I can't bear it. For three days, we walked through the maize fields and those plants cut our faces to pieces.

'When I got to Venice, I was lucky because my sister was already here. She was looking after an old lady who was senile, so she could smuggle me into the house at night, to sleep. In the days, I would walk around the city looking for work. Or I would sit in the parks.

'Then, someone – I don't know – a neighbour or another Moldovan maybe – told the old woman's daughter, about me, so I had to leave that house. Other Moldovan women took me in. I stayed in many different places. There is a whole network of Moldovans working in this city. Some are good people; some are not. Like everywhere. I have known some very good people and some very bad people in my life.'

The Eastern European housekeepers and carers gather in the park near to our house every Sunday afternoon. They sit on the benches under the tall lime trees. At first I do not distinguish these respectable-looking middle-aged women, gossiping on the benches, from any other Italian matrons of the same age. Then, as I am walking with the children to the playground one day, I see two women, one of whom is brushing the other's hair, and I looked closer.

Italians only do what they consider to be *outside* things in public. They do not eat on the street, except for ice creams; they do not do their hair, except perhaps to flick it back glamorously or pat it into place. They emerge from their houses turned out for public, not private, life. They are made up, buttoned up, ready to face the day-lit world. There is, therefore, something disconcertingly intimate – almost, you might say, naked – about these ageing women hairdressing on the park bench.

That is when I realize that they are not Italian at all; that they do not have comfortably besuited husbands in tow, or grandchildren in buggies; they only have each other. And of course, this is when I notice that they are physically different too: heavier, more solid, with square faces and fairer complexions and staider, cheaper clothes. They are from Romania, Moldova, Uzbekistan, Kyrgyzstan and other ex-Soviet countries, and they are in Venice to work.

On another Sunday afternoon, I watch a small group of these women standing in a circle near the stone fountain and singing. As they sing, they bow rhythmically to each other and clap their hands in time to the melody. I feel sure that this is the ghost of a dance they would, under other, more relaxed circumstances, marry to their rousing, repetitive, defiant and melancholy anthem.

The same women appear on warm evenings near our local

vaporetto stop. They sit their ample behinds on the stone ledge of the raised *campo* that looks out across the Grand Canal. Placed at intervals between them are wheelchairs, in which droop the ancient wisps of human beings for whom they care. The women chatter and laugh over the heads of their fragile charges and I detect shreds of cruelty – relief at being able to disregard their duty and talk in their own language; at being, for now, in the majority, free to gossip about home and their resentments.

The Life of Fish

The mansions arranged along either bank of the canal made one think of objects of nature, but of a nature which seemed to have created its works with a human imagination.

(Marcel Proust, *Albertine disparue*)

CITIES BANK UP buildings and bodies as insurance against decay. When one individual falls by the wayside, ten more step forward to fill the gap. Cities make us feel good because the city that never sleeps is, by a kind of illogical extension, the place where you never die; the lights are always on, the conversation and the wine flow for ever.

But when you dig – down, down, down – what do you find? Under the patterned labyrinths of medieval ghettos and the Roman pavements; below the woven huts and the undulating palisades are the marshlands, the scrublands and the unconstructed world.

In most cities, this is what we can only imagine, seeing in the glimpsed face of an urban fox an ancient order stealthily recolonizing. But in Venice you need make no such effort of the imagination. When the *acqua alta* is seriously high, what strikes me is not the rainbow lake, a city afloat on reflections, but the mudwash, the drain-disgorgement: the rise and rise of filth.

For centuries before any thought of global warming, these periodic inundations would have come as a portent of apocalypse. What had already happened long ago, in the biblical past, would, with terrifying inevitability, happen again one day in the future. Then, the city that had come out of the primordial slime would disappear, submerged forever by the waters. But for now, every time the tides skulk away, the clouds clear and Venice, this most perfect of human ornaments, glistens again – ancient and reborn – in the sunlight. And it is partly because of this rising and falling of waters, this prominence of natural processes, that you never lose sight of the artistry of the place, of the fact that it is a constructed thing.

What one can forget, though, is that this beautiful artefact is set against other lives: the life of fish, the arrivals and departures of birds and of itinerant human beings; the sudden impasse of the mudflat. Waiting for a *vaporetto* on the Grand Canal, I remember that I am in the middle of a salt water lagoon when a silver fish flops out of the water, or a quick little shoal flickers by below my feet.

The lone fisherman, standing over there, in the shadow of a tremendous palace, casting his rod on a summer's evening, is a part of that other world too. If you take care to look closely, this parallel life is revealed more than you might expect.

My friend Jenny is walking among the stone pines at the easternmost tip of the city. A little way off she sees a group of unassuming elderly men and women in tracksuits, training binoculars on the tree canopy above their heads.

'I knew they were British,' she tells me afterwards, 'and I went up to ask them what they were doing.'

They are, it turns out, a party of Lancashire twitchers who have just left the Po Delta where they have been watching the arrival of the migrating birds. On their way home, they decide to stop off in Venice where, because they are twitchers before anything, they quickly leave behind the splendours of Piazza San Marco and the Rialto bridge and come to this out-of-the-way nineteenth-century quarter, devoid of medieval palazzi, but with a significant arboreal canopy in which a rare, red tree creeper has recently been spotted. They are not, as they wander through the park with their binoculars, really *tourists* at all,

171

but something practically unheard of in Venice these days: they are travellers, passing through on their way to somewhere else.

My friend, pleased by this, thinks of something that might interest them.

'There's another unusual bird around here,' she says, 'I've never heard of one of these before. It's an albino blackbird!'

The twitchers lower their binoculars; they smile at her politely; they are unmoved.

'Yes,' they say, 'we know.'

And they are so very separate from the world of mass tourism or luxury tourism and all the other tourisms, that they seem, miraculously somehow, to have drifted in on another current. Like the fish, like the birds and the tide.

In the spring, the swallows arrive in the city. In rural Britain there has been such a rush to restore old barns in the last few years that these small birds have often been fatally deprived of the elevated nesting places they need. When a tumbledown garage outside my house was demolished, the practically legless creatures swooped low through the new windows and became frantically shipwrecked on the furniture, in the folds of curtains. Loss of habitat can hardly be a problem in Venice with its acres of ramshackle belfries and crumbling ledges, and when they arrive they flood in, shrill, like little roaring boys – skirmishing, wheeling, minuscule flying aces. The space between the buildings outside my kitchen window is their diving pool. They swoop, circle and call, slicing back and forth in their lovely element, up and down, turning, gliding across the sky prairie. They occupy it, cross-hatch and navigate and possess the area with their small, fleet selves.

When the window is open, I can hear their wings cut through the hot air. There is a twittering, cheaping, chirping cacophony. The gulls – off stage – squabble like gangs of jungle monkeys. Sometimes, a big pigeon flaps comfortably by, dense wings beating heavily through the stillness.

And then, the bronze bells begin to clang and Venice's concert of the air comes crowding in, a world of space and dissonant music.

*

There are other migrants who arrive and briefly stay. Coming home from the market, I pass over a bridge and see a group of African street vendors. Tall, elegant men leaning loosely against the wall, their wares – fake designer bags and sunglasses – bundled up in white sheets, at their feet. They are talking and laughing in a language I do not recognize. Then, suddenly, without a word passing between them – but as if an electric current has, in that moment, been switched on – they grab up their bundles and leg it: bounding away, skimming off at angles down different alleys, fleeing the still invisible police, and as they scatter, they break into exuberant laughter and disappear, instantly.

This sudden flight is no game, but these men live it like one and it is impossible not to smile.

In the winter, there is another, small and quiet human migration – men from, I guess, Indonesia. They squat in the streets and construct models of grasshoppers and frogs out of reeds. As they finish each small, ephemeral masterpiece, they hang it on a branch propped beside them in a bottle.

The grasshopper men sit on their haunches in an easy squat that is as alien to a European physicality, a Western sensibility, as the gypsy women's prostration on cold stone.

Their deft-fingered craft, the simplicity of the material, the absolute pre-industrial quality of what they are doing, makes of them, to my eyes and in my world, something fragile and rare.

Like the Africans, like the gypsies, they are economic migrants, at the bottom of the great pile of European riches, but they have none of the others' apparent strengths of speed or wily, dogged determination. They just squat and twist and make their little spidery marvels for a few euros apiece.

When I see a policeman moving one of these grasshopper men along from his corner pitch by the bridge of the Guglie, I cannot imagine why this absurd dislodging should need to happen. Venice, the city, is only real and only has value for as long as there are many lives being lived in it: the lives of fishes, the lives of children, the lives of wheedling gypsies and quarrelsome gulls, the twitchers and fishermen, the swallows and the Africans – primed for instant flight and laughter.

It's only a matter of luck where you wash up in history. What was once Babylon is now Baghdad.

For the whole morning, a drunk has been sitting slumped on the bridge below my window. He sits down there still, calling out, almost cheerfully, to no one in particular or perhaps to all of Venice:

'Coraggio … coraggio … coraggio …'

Sunday 25 May

It is a hot and cloudless morning and we are heading out of the city in Giampaolo's boat, chopping across the glittering water, towards the open Lagoon.

Our small craft is stuffed with children, picnic baskets, wine, swimming costumes, hats, sun cream, water bottles, towels and fishing nets and buckets – all the accoutrements of beach life that make us into travellers for a day, our camp on our backs. We are not alone; all around us there are dozens of small boats also setting off. The Lagoon is Venice's countryside; this is the Venetian equivalent of a Sunday walk in the country.

The Venetian archipelago is made up of over fifty islands. Some, like San Secondo melting pathetically away by the Ponte della Libertà, barely exist any more; others have disappeared entirely, leaving only a name and, perhaps, an occasionally emerging sandbank. Almost all are in a state of radical decay, their shorelines nibbled away, year in year out, by the tides; their buildings – convents, monasteries, churches, hospitals, villas, boatyards – either gone or ruined.

The long, slow death of the islands of the Lagoon began 200 years ago with the occupation of the city by Napoleon in 1797 and the death of the Republic. For a thousand years, each island, many of them very small indeed, had played its part in the ecosystem of the Lagoon and the infrastructure of the Venetian Republic. Many of them housed a monastic community, each one of which was obliged by law to include in its complex of buildings a gunpowder tower. By keeping these

THE POLITICS OF WASHING

potentially incendiary stores in isolation, the Republic could be sure of having adequate reserves of gunpowder while, at the same time, remaining safe from the potentially devastating effect of an explosion in the densely populated city itself.

Then there were the fishing islands and farming islands and, crucially, as trade grew and the flow of people entering the city from all over the world increased in the age of plagues, the hospital and quarantine islands. Venice has the oldest public health system in the Western world and it is no accident that the word 'quarantine' was coined here. In the glory days of the Republic, with ships arriving from almost every part of the known world, it was imperative for the Venetians to devise a way of limiting the spread of disease, most particularly the Black Death. It was, therefore, made mandatory for incoming ships to stop at quarantine islands and for the crew and passengers to sit out forty (*quaranta*) days, until it was clear they were not carrying the plague. I wonder about those unfortunate sailors and merchants who arrived perfectly healthy and were then forced to stay forty days cheek by jowl with those already infected.

Then Napoleon came and, in a dual drive to castrate the dying Republic and impose the French system of secular governance, instigated a mass closure of the monasteries. Treasures were removed, glorious buildings emptied and either demolished or left to fall into disrepair; military installations were constructed in their place. Nowadays, on the island of Certosa, for example, there is no visible trace of the Carthusian order and the magnificent church they finished building there in 1492. But the French military lookout posts remain: a series of dour, geometrical little sentinel boxes dotted along the shoreline.

Napoleon's systematic ruination of these jewels of architecture and art in the Lagoon is surely one of the greatest acts of cultural destruction in history. The thought of it, 200 years later, makes my blood boil.

On this summer Sunday, our little boat goes deeper into this world of ghostly islands as Giampaolo steers us away from the crowds and we enter the canal that bisects the island of Poveglia. Once in the narrow thoroughfare, the sense of movement and wind and light instantly disappears and we are passing through sultry, enclosed waters. On either side of us, the banks are overgrown with brambles and the air is full of raucous insects.

It is time for lunch, so we tie the boat to a large, rusting iron ring set into the marble blocks that shore up the sides of the canal and recall another, grander and worldly past for this small, deserted island. The white stone, the silence, the riot of brambles: we might be deep in the jungle, could have stumbled across the remains of an ancient civilization.

We eat our picnic in the baking stillness, our rug spread out on the landing stage, in the shade of tired acacia trees. We talk about the future of the city. It is the same familiar conversation that Venice has over and over again with itself. It goes like this: here we are, living in the most wonderful place imaginable – not merely for its evident beauty, but for the inestimable privilege of a daily life without cars. And yet, we desperately need more people to live here, *really* live here, so that it can come fully alive again. The foreigners who buy apartments and come for a week every so often add nothing to the place. This disaster that is uncontrolled tourism is destroying daily life in the city, and this quality of life is quite as precious, quite as much a treasure of the human race, as the palaces and bell towers and canals taken hostage by the tour guides. Perhaps more so. What can we do? What can we do?

When we have finished eating, feeling hot and full and dispirited, I get up and wander off on my own, following a dirt track into the mess of undergrowth behind us. I step over fallen tree trunks, squeeze between saplings, and duck under brambles until I come to a clearing and the buildings and church tower I glimpsed earlier from the boat. This is the remains of the quarantine hospital which, though now a virtual ruin, is an early twentieth-century addition to the island whose history stretches back more than 1,200 years.

I make my way gingerly over the heaps of white rubble towards a gaping doorway. I look through into what must once have been the hospital kitchen. There is an industrial-sized, stainless steel cooker lying upended with its four feet in the air and several enormous aluminium pans are scattered around the floor. It's the giant's palace again.

The terracotta floor is intact but the plaster ceiling hangs in a dry swag, like a crumbling stage curtain, and I can see straight up to the floor above. A soft drizzle of plaster powders my hair as I walk, as though I have set off an imperceptible tremor just by being there. I wonder how safe this place is, but I am too curious to go back.

The hospital is built around a central courtyard. Most of the wooden doors have been barricaded shut, but when I peer through cracks, I see that the rooms are ruined shells. There is a wide flight of splintered wooden stairs leading up to the first floor. This, I do not risk. The sawing of crickets intensifies the silence. The air is alive with mosquitoes and I am constantly brushing them away from my face and arms. Now, I feel like the prince who has cut his way through the enchanted forest to Sleeping Beauty's castle. But this time it is deserted; I have come too late.

Back at the landing stage, the others are packing up the picnic.

'Let's go for a swim,' says Giampaolo, and I am content to leave this melancholy place and join the cheerful banality of a day at the beach.

The beach he has in mind is, however, not just any beach: it is uniquely Venetian, which is to say that, most of the time, it is knee deep in water and therefore invisible. Its whereabouts are known only to locals, and it is only accessible by private boat. On summer days, people from the city go there in their droves. You know you have arrived because the spot is marked by many small vessels, like a flock of seabirds, wings folded, bobbing peacefully together on the water.

And the owners of these boats have, in their turn, become long-leg-ged waders. Though the elderly or indolent may stay put, reading the paper or sunbathing in the bows, most people get out and do the usual beach things – playing ball, having water fights, chatting to friends – and all of it calf-deep in water.

Every so often, at a certain point in the tide's ebb and flow, a sand-bank emerges from the shallows and this is instantly colonized by beach umbrellas, tables and chairs. Within minutes, whole families are to be seen perched on a narrow ridge of sand, eating lunch or playing cards. It is the unlikely and surreal opposite of an oasis in the desert. And the inhabitants of Venice who, it seems to me, do have something amphibian about them, whether they are browsing in a flooded bookshop or playing catch, up to their knees in salt water, are, after all, still hanging on in here and relishing their strange home for all they are worth.

PART 11: June

Home and Away

FOR CENTURIES PEOPLE have come to Venice looking for another, new version of themselves, a reinvention of their prosaic daily self through the extravagant theatricality of the city. What these visitors choose to wear exposes and enhances their fantasies.

On the whole, Venetians adopt uniformly monochrome, understated and practical clothes. What distinguishes the rich from the rest is not necessarily style (why would one wear anything other than sensible shoes and trousers in a place where you simply have to walk everywhere?), so much as label and quality of garment. Nothing differentiates a visitor from a local more than a pair of high heels.

During the first week of the Biennale, the international art show that takes place in Venice every two years, I notice that some of those who have come for the event are struggling with certain contradictions between what they are and where they are. One bright June morning, as I am walking down the long, wide Fondamenta della Misericordia, I see three men coming out of one of the exhibition spaces, a little way ahead of me. The exhibit is about buildings and I get the impression that they are all architects, albeit of quite different provenance.

Two of them might be brothers or, at the very least, brothers in arms. They are tall, meaty men; they have thin, reddish hair and reddish skin; they both wear immaculately pressed pink and white checked, short-sleeved cotton shirts, with what look like air vents set into the sleeves near the shoulder. Their cream-coloured slacks have many zipped pockets and their plain brown brogues are polished to a military shine. Their gait is slow and somehow manages to be loose-limbed and rather stiff at the same time. They remind me of my Uncle Brian, a big, gentle sheep farmer from the Western District of Victoria in Australia. I am sure that they, too, are Australian.

The third man, their companion, is altogether a different animal. He is small and slight, with a fine mane of wavy black hair swept back artistically from his high forehead. He wears a fashionably cut black suit, a black shirt and a black tie, and the total effect is elegantly insouciant. He walks alongside his large, pink companions, gesturing showily, but nervously, as he talks. I cannot hear what he is saying, but imagine that he is an Italian architect guiding his antipodean colleagues around the Biennale. Curious to know if I have read the cultural signs accurately, I quicken my pace and come up close enough behind them to eavesdrop their conversation.

Yes, the big men, as I guessed, are Australian. They are talking slowly and appreciatively about the exhibition they have just seen. I was also right about the nerves of the little man in black, which are certainly highly wrought – he speaks fast and emphatically, as though dancing on verbal hot coals. But I was wrong in supposing him Italian. It is true that this is the impression he wishes to give: the gorgeous maestro's hair-do, the unstyled yet stylish suit. Nature has helped him in this too – he is wiry and olive complexioned – but his accent is unambiguously Australian.

I feel for the man in the black suit, so visibly ill-at-ease that his almost perfect European cover is being blown by these two big, pink, colonial appendages with whom he is obliged to walk. It occurs to me that, in an ironic little back flip of history, he might in fact be of Italian descent. It is more than possible that some generations earlier, his forebears, exhausted by poverty and lack of hope in their village in Calabria or Campania or Sicily, boarded the big ship to the other side of the world, in search of the good life. It is more than possible, too, that the family made its way back from the brink of desperation, through hard work and a new-found optimism, and began to flourish, so that, perhaps half a century later, here he is, one of their descendants, back again: a successful Sydney architect, visiting the Venetian Biennale in an Armani suit.

The bluff country architects with whom he is travelling come, most probably, from less ravaged, more prosperous beginnings. I imagine that those ambling, big-boned men, with their bright blue eyes and fair skin, are, like me, the descendants of burly Scotsmen, who set off for the Australian Gold Fields, and set up shop as grocers or wheelwrights or railway contractors: determined and hardy people, with an eye to a profit, made on the back of an unflinching Protestant work ethic.

Somewhere along the line, lots of things have got muddled together. Now, what counts is cool, is image, not mere hard graft. And the seeds of this highly prized glamour are to be found not in the Highlands, but in the bone-dry olive groves of the South.

Later the same day, I am on the *vaporetto*. It is packed to the bulwarks: the seats inside are full of tourists, gazing quietly out of the windows with rapt expressions as the palaces of the Grand Canal slip by. Because they got on the boat at the beginning of its run, at Piazzale Roma, they have taken up all the seats. The people who are standing stuffed along the aisles are in a less blissful state of mind and are mostly Venetians. Some are muttering dark imprecations against the tourists who have colonized the seating. The tourists remain happily unaware of the bile emanating from their fellow passengers. There is a stench of sweat and the oppression of too many bodies.

Lurching through the water, under the weight of its cargo of placid tourists and irritable Venetians, the *vaporetto* veers lumberingly towards the landing stage at Rialto Mercato. Strangely, surreally, for this busy time of year, there is only one person waiting on the platform: a young man, of simply gargantuan dimensions. He is as wide as three people. He has that smooth, babyish look of the obese, however old they are. He could only be American – and this not only because of his size. He stands there with his little round glasses, his hands hanging loose by his sides, his sneakered toes turned out, in his enormous tee-shirt, his enormous jeans, and observes, with the smallest and sweetest of smiles, the approaching vessel that is so inordinately, burstingly full of people. And I cannot say whether it is a smile of resignation, of denial or of despair.

I am getting off soon and have already begun the slow shove towards the front. It wouldn't be the first time I've got stuck and the *vaporetto* has chugged on to the next stop before I can squeeze myself out of the boat. That happened in the days before I learnt how you do it: first, repeatedly call out a loud and insistent: 'Permesso!' ('Excuse me!') and then, resorting to unashamed elbowing, force the wall of bodies to part and let you through.

As I step off the boat there is, ahead of me, a young and strikingly handsome couple. They are both slim and tall and ineffably glamorous. The man, who is a few steps in front, has on a beautiful pale linen suit which he wears over a subtly coloured shirt, open at the collar. His silky blond hair falls in a perfect lock over his tanned forehead; he strolls with both hands in his pockets and is, every inch of him, careless, East Coast American aristocracy. As I slow down behind him, he turns back languidly to his wife to ask her, 'Are you OK?'

She is patently not OK.

The woman is dark, where he is blond. Her hair is sleekly bobbed, her lips impeccable scarlet; her little, cream silk shift dress is a mere accompaniment to her physical loveliness. She comes along the gangplank on the most disappearing of strappy, high heeled sandals, but what is striking about her is not this predictable beauty, her magazine style, nor that of her husband; what is striking is the massive baby in her ballet dancer's arms. There it is: a great cube of infancy, in stripy dungarees, with wisps of mousy hair and a face smeared with chocolate ice cream. There it is with its fat hands and its bulging fists, its one sock on and one sock off, its impossible weight and its unworkable wriggliness. By the look of it, it was born about a year ago. By the look of her, this is absolutely the first time ever, coming en famille to the Venice Biennale, that she has had to pick the thing up and deal with it.

Beside the Seaside, Beside the Sea

WHAT CHARMS ME when I first arrive in Venice is the illusion of class-lessness. The absence of cars, the absolute necessity of using your feet to get from one place to another, has a wonderfully levelling effect because, on the street, you are mixing with people from every walk of life. The only private transport other than a baby buggy that exists here is the boat, but by no means everybody owns one and a mooring close to home can be very difficult to find. Those people who have both a boat and parking for it come from every section of society, because getting hold of a mooring is not a question of mere money but also one of contacts and address, perseverance and, on occasion, guile.

Sometimes, rich foreigners come to Venice and use water taxis as they would an SUV at home, but they miss the point and cut a clumsy and ridiculous figure in this city whose own rich and important are regularly to be seen walking from one place to another, just like every-body else.

The grace of Venice lies in its fluidity. Except for the days when you've got a washing machine to remove from the fourth floor, this world of footsteps is easy and pleasurable to navigate. It can also allow for friendly and unexpected contact across barriers of class and money. In this, as in much else, Venice is a happy anachronism in the Western world and has some resemblance, perhaps, to eight-eenth-century London, where the elegant, aristocratic town houses of Soho crowded in, side by side, with coffee houses and inns, shops and brothels; or ancient cities, like Pompeii, where a modern visitor is surprised to find that the entrance to the most luxurious of patrician villas is an unassuming door stuck between an oil merchant's and a barber's shop.

But all this convivial mixing comes to an abrupt end every year, on 1 June. This is the day the beach huts or *capanne* open on the Lido, Venice's very own beach island. This is the day that the mass migration of the city's population from street to strand begins to gather momen-tum, reaching its pitch in July.

*

The Venetian year is marked out by certain traditional events, most of which are linked to religion: the feast of the Redentore and the pilgrimage to the Salute, San Martino and the brief, delicious appearance of *fritelle*, the little carnival fritters, in the cake shops in February. But one of the main events in the city's calendar is unashamedly secular: it is the *capanna* season.

We devotees of the Lido in winter are in a definite minority. The long spit of sand is not the most beautiful beach in the world. On a grey afternoon in January, with the icy Bora blowing in from the northeast, the empty hotels, the boarded-up bars and mess of half-finished developments along the edge of the sea, it is nothing short of Soviet. But for all that, on a winter Sunday, the short ferry ride across the Lagoon, a brisk stride beside the Adriatic, and lunch in a trattoria, is the Venetian version of a walk in the country and a pub lunch. As the dank city begins to close in during those empty weeks after Christmas, there is relief in the wider skies, and those of us in need of it return home across the Lagoon on Sunday evenings, our heads cleared out by the wind and the space and ready for another week in the stone labyrinth.

But between June and September any hope of a brisk stride on the beach is mere fantasy. The Lido is colonized by thousands of painted huts, springing up, so it seems, overnight, like so many polka dots on a bikini. These huts are about the size of a garden shed, with a little roofed porch section on the front where one can sit outside, perhaps at a table or on a deck chair. Inside, there is a wooden bench that runs around the walls, some hooks for your clothes, and a curtain that can be pulled across to make a private changing room. And that is all.

The *capanne* are arranged in neat rows. The front row is, of course, the most desirable and the most expensive, having an unblocked sea view. Temporary plastic walkways are laid out between the huts, in a grid, so that one can visit friends or relatives or go to the bar or toilet block barefoot, without touching the scorching sand. It is hard to believe that the windswept reaches of the winter beach are the same place when you are walking around these little impromptu, gridded metropolises that owe more to Mondrian than de Chirico.

On opening day, the city's population arrives, hauling and lugging their kit for a summer on the beach. They stow away swimming costumes, towels, ointments and sprays and sandals and sarongs in their little wooden houses.

So far, so united, but that's the last glimpse anyone has of the Republic of the *Calli*. Each day, throughout the summer, *vaporetti* disgorge thousands of citizens at the Lido. Once off the boat, everyone makes their way up the central street, the Gran Viale, towards the beach, which lies on the other, Adriatic, side of the island. The Gran Viale is not, it must be said, very grand; it is a street of average length, lined with bars and ice cream shops, beachwear purveyors and pizzerias. There are a few cars and lots of bicycles; tables and chairs are set out on the pavement under pergolas of wisteria, roses and jasmine. It is a busy little promenade, full of holiday promise and people of all ages, strolling, licking ice creams, gossiping. I like it; it reminds me of a musical hall song we used to sing as children, already antiquated in the 1960s:

'Oh I do like to be beside the seaside, oh I do like to be beside the sea!' But, for all its holiday atmosphere, the Gran Viale is the place where the sheep are sorted out from the goats – the rich from the poor, the aristocrat from the plebeian, from the bourgeois. The Gran Viale, that short strip of street, so anonymous, so comfortably unclassy, so much in the festive mode, is like a passage along which one must travel from the fantasy world of La Serenissima, in order to be born, brutally, into a tougher, more real world of insuperable class distinctions. As Venice surges, in sunhats and Ray Bans, towards the sea, along this most provincial of promenades, she ceases to be the City of Dreams and becomes Every Town. Why? Well, it's all in the zone.

Every summer, the long Lido beach is divided up into sections called zones. Each one is managed separately as a sort of family holiday camp, with bars, showers, toilet blocks, table tennis, games for small children and, of course, the *capanne*. But before describing the different zones in more detail, I must first confess my shoddy, freeloading credentials.

When I arrive in Venice, I cannot for the life of me understand why the locals cough up such exorbitant sums of money every summer for a beach hut. The cheapest zones boast *capanne* at the knockdown rental of 5,000 euros for the three-month season, while the classiest will provide you with the same wooden hut (though acres more distant from your neighbours, and with superior furnishings) for a mere 15,000 euros. For those to whom 5,000 euros for a beach hut represents a serious budgetary challenge, the solution is clear: you go in on a *capanna* with every single relation, friend, passer-by you can collar on the street. So that, as is always the way, the housing of the poor is chronically overcrowded: the 'cheaper' zones are heaving with people, and on hot weekends are not unlike the Favelas of São Paolo.

Surely, I thought when I first arrived in Venice, the sea belongs to Everyman, and anyway I couldn't see the attraction of decamping from your narrow street and apartment block to another narrow street (sand not stone), along with most of the same neighbours (albeit arranged horizontally rather than vertically and wearing many fewer clothes). So I bought myself a beach umbrella and went walkabout, sometimes setting up camp on the no-man's-land of the *spiaggia libera*, or Free Beach, where students, immigrants and creepy lone men hang out, sometimes visiting friends in one or other of the different zones.

One of the advantages of being a foreigner anywhere can be a sort of social fluidity – it is often less easy to put foreigners into boxes. As a result, perhaps, I have friends in *all* the zones. I have spent long, hot afternoons between the rows of oiled, baking and oozing matrons and their tumbling grandchildren, in the jolly populous and popular zones; I have enjoyed the busy, but less cramped, family atmosphere of the bourgeois middle-range zones and I have (secretly) relished the silken sand and open spaces of the top-of-the-range zone, despite deciding early on that I could not afford to be seen in a bikini among that many beautiful, hungry people.

Yes, I was that ignominious creature, a hutless beach-goer, a permanent outsider. And yet, now some time into my Venetian life, I have to admit to a Sea Change. Not into something Rich and Strange, but into something Poor and Aspirational. There are days when I find myself wishing that I too had a *capanna*. Not just any *capanna*, but a *capanna* in the Top Zone. That I could be a part of all that shiny, exclusive beach stuff. That I, too, could have a cane lounger with fat cream cushions and a view of the Adriatic uncluttered by a heaving mass of bodies. Because, you must believe me, the extraordinary thing is that when you are in the Top Zone, even the sea looks different – more, somehow, Caribbean – and the furnishings are indubitably softer.

Which is why I can see that it's time for me to move on: time to accept that class distinctions are alive and well in Paradise and that one cannot slough off one's roots, that we all have a place on the Lido, and that mine is not in the zones. I must abjure my beach umbrella, turn my back on the *capanne*, and retreat to the distant reaches of the Lido, where there is not even a beach; where the avant-garde set have hauled driftwood and debris from the Adriatic and used it to build wonderful platforms and fragile, curlicued structures on the white stones of the breakwater; where some inspired wag has created palm trees from salt-bleached tree trunks, hung with the flotsam of Fanta bottles, and set up an alternative biennale of beach art, made from anything they could reclaim from the sea, for discriminating passers-by. Here, in the long summer evenings, the people lie about in hammocks, in a bohemian and creative kind of way, drinking prosecco and gazing out to sea, thinking about Art and Utopia.

Opus Dei

MY FATHER AND I used to get up early and, with J. G. Links's famous guide *Venice for Pleasure* in hand, go off to explore the city. I remember the still, clear mornings of those childhood holidays in Venice, and my father, who loved the amiable, rambling J. G. like a brother, reading aloud to me all the way, barely drawing breath to look up at the buildings and views to which the book was leading us. What mattered most, after all, were not the stones of the city, but the smell of the early morning air, the sunshine and the companionship of a father and daughter, walking together before breakfast.

Now, thirty-five years later, actually living in the city, I spend my days walking past those monuments and curiosities to school meetings and work appointments; to have coffee with a friend; to get to the farmers' market and the doctor's surgery. Art and culture really do not figure in my domestic routine, unless you count the school concerts and the fancy pastries. Which is why, after almost a year, I begin to feel vaguely guilty about the sheer quantity of art I have *not* looked at since I became a resident of Venice.

One hot June afternoon, I decide to do something about this and go to look at a painting by one of my favourite Renaissance painters, Lorenzo Lotto, whose physically solid and psychologically subtle portraits of traders and scholars feel to me so vividly Venetian. It is to be found in a nearby church.

As I set out through the city, everything seems unusually still; it is the heat that I hear, not the familiar soft bustle of footsteps and voices. When I arrive in Campo Santa Margherita I understand why: Italy is playing Slovakia in the Football World Cup. The four or five bars in the area have rigged up flat-screen televisions on the pavement and each screen is surrounded by a crowd of people, seated and standing, all watching the game intently.

As I pass through a bottleneck between two of these groups, Italy scores a goal. A great roar of elation bursts from the crowd as though a curling wave has risen magically up from the stones of the *campo* and is carrying us all forward for a brief, glorious moment of shared joy. Even I, alone, accidentally present and with no interest in football, find myself grinning broadly, swept up in the emotion that surrounds me. Then the referee decides against allowing the goal and the spectators yell and gesture passionately at the screens – arms outstretched, hands splayed, as though flinging the referee's decision back in his face.

I leave the football behind me and walk on to the church which sits on the other side of the *campo*. It is a big old place, like an outbuilding on an aristocratic estate, where the family has dumped its unwanted furniture and works of art over generations. The sun, streaming in through high windows, is thick with dust motes and illuminates unlikely tangles of brass work, ramshackle chairs and tables, and blackened oil paintings lost in magnificently pompous gilt frames. It is handsome, shabby, familiar and neglected.

As I step in from the baking outside world, the church feels cool and quiet. There is hardly anybody around. Close up to the altar, a stocky elderly woman sits in a pew; she is rocking heavily back and forth, her feet pacing out a strangely nimble repeating pattern, first on the lower wooden bar of the pew in front and then back on the floor. She mutters noisily to herself as she moves – whether in prayer, or in some disturbed, obsessive mantra of her own, I cannot tell.

On the other side of the aisle, some way behind the swaying woman, there sits a skinny old man in a black suit. He is writing intently in a notebook balanced on his knee. After a while, he gets up and goes to the lectern, where the Bible is spread open on golden eagle's wings. Perhaps he too is mad, I think, and is on the point of declaiming from the scriptures, at the top of his voice, to the almost empty church. But he says nothing and it occurs to me that it is I, not the old man or the rocking woman, who is off course: one of the banal godless, capable of suspecting that the devout or the contemplative might be touched not by faith but by insanity.

I amble around the church, looking idly for the Lotto. It is nowhere to be seen and I eventually realize that it is hidden behind scaffolding and sheets, in a side chapel. It is, not unusually for this land of endless restoration work, *in restauro* and hidden from sight. I don't much care and wander on, aimlessly.

Two workmen, in plaster-splattered overalls, stride quickly past me up the central aisle talking as though they are in the street, so that their chat is unnaturally amplified in the still, contained space of the church. They disappear through the sacristy door.

Next, a young man rushes in through a side entrance.

'One all!' he calls out excitedly to the rocking woman.

'Ha!' she says, continuing to rock.

Then another explosive roar comes up from the *campo*, distant now, but ferocious in its passion. The young man, who is painfully thin, his pale face inflamed with acne, turns abruptly back towards the open door and casts an anguished look out to the *campo*, where the action is, hopelessly torn between his duties in the church and his burning desire to be back in the hot, sunlit world of the football match.

This is when the priest rounds the corner, walking swiftly and neatly in his black cassock, a shiny leather briefcase slotted under one arm, his white hair cut close around his face. He takes one look at the boy and understands the situation.

'Vai!' he says sharply, 'Go!' and the young man, unfrozen by this reprieve, this benediction, sprints out of the church and races across the *campo*, to join the crowd.

Part 12: July

Itinerant

I DON'T KNOW if there are more tourists here in this hottest month, but there are certainly many fewer Venetians, so the sense in the city of being overrun is at its height. That and the effort of dragging one's overheated body through the sometimes insufferable heat.

There is one man I notice walking about the area in these dog days. At first he seems, like all the other tourists, to be following a set itinerary, walking along the *fondamenta*, dressed in shorts and trainers, with a small rucksack slung over his shoulder, a camera around his neck, his face tanned. But then I notice him a second and a third time in the course of several days, repeating, it seems, the same itinerary over and over again. This is when I realize that his tan is not of the smooth, holiday variety, the seasonal badge of well-heeled leisure, but is darker, deeper, rougher. His trainers are scuffed and spreading from long, hard use, and I see that as he walks along the *fondamenta* he is not gazing around, star struck by the fairytale city, but has the closed-off, inward look of a survivor.

Although he neither smiles nor appears to relate in any obvious way to Venice, the old lag, masquerading as day tripper, spends his wandering hours enacting, in his very person, as consummate and tragic a piece of satire as you could hope to find anywhere on the streets of this city that has become a slave to tourism.

In the winter of 2010, a sixty-one-year-old tramp was set on fire. His name was Marino Scarpa and he described himself as a Venetian DOC – that increasingly rare creature. For some years and despite attempts to persuade him to do otherwise, he slept rough in an out-of-the-way courtyard. During the winter, his home was a hut of cardboard boxes.

One night, a group of teenagers gathered in the courtyard and started to hurl abuse at him. They were, he later said, between fifteen and seventeen years old and themselves DOC Venetians. They took cigarette lighters out of their pockets and began trying to set fire to Scarpa's cardboard boxes. Finally, the flames took and he also found that the arm of his coat was alight. Terrified, he managed to put the flame out and to run away.

Like the clown-tourist, wandering the *fondamentas* of the city, it seems to me that this ugly desecration has shades of the morality play – the final, ghastly chapter in the Venetian fairy tale in which the young natives ritually, barbarically slay the goose that lays their golden egg.

Pinhole Camera

'If Venice sinks, future generations will know what she looks like.'
(J. G. Links)

IT TAKES THE best part of a morning for my father-in-law, *il nonno*, to set up his home movies. Two dusty cardboard boxes must be humped up from the storeroom in the basement of the building. He lifts an antiquated projector out of a nest of yellowing newspapers; the cords are stiffly uncoiled; the screen unfurled; and the projector is set on a little tower of magazines. The generous, old-fashioned reels of celluloid are dusted down and then clicked into place on the projector.

Now he is ready and the family is summoned. The adults are ranged along the sofa in a straight line, knees just touching; children sit on the floor. It is a temporarily ordered version of family life. The blinds on the big windows are lowered mechanically, clacking down, slat against slat, until we are in a pitch darkness that only gradually calibrates to dusk. The projector refuses to start. Nonno adjusts it again. Somebody, bored with waiting, fretful about the lunch, nips out to the kitchen and is called back urgently. Then comes the quick-flickering of black strokes on a white void; nonsense hieroglyphs; fossilized insect skeletons which flower suddenly into intense, staccato images of a lost present.

A young woman walks briskly across our frame of view. She is dark-haired, her curving black eyebrows are expressive against her white skin. Her skirt is just above the knee, low enough to tell us that she is a respectable Italian wife and mother, high enough to confirm that the year is 1966 or thereabouts. She is the younger self of the stout old lady who sits, a little slumped, beside me on the sofa, her bronchitic lungs labouring even in repose. The young woman glances out from her sunny alpine day forty years ago and then turns away, without recognition or foreboding, because where she is, is now, and what she is looking around for is not the future, but her two small sons.

Meanwhile, Nonno, the proud projectionist, informs us that these are the Alps, and the shot pans crawlingly across immemorial white peaks.

'But where's Daddy?' one of the children asks from the floor.

Nonno does not seem to hear the question, being intent on the ticking reel, the fractional, technical adjustments of focus and speed.

Now, we see a scattering of alpine chalets, their lattice-carved balconies and windowboxes dense with the scarlet scribble of geraniums; then, flower-specked meadows; then, again, the so-slowly-unfolding, so icily eternal, Alps, filmed from left to right, then back again, from right to left. That masterly, unflinching hand-held camera shot is all that remains of Nonno's thirty-five-year-old Alpha male self.

'But where's Dad?' The members of the front row insist.

They want to see their father become one of them. They want to see him playing as they play. They want to meet those two young brothers – their father and uncle, the two middle-aged men on the sofa – magically restored to childhood. But we, the obedient, captive audience, continue to glide with the camera across the limpid surface of a glacial lake. We see the surrounding peaks reflected in glassy water. We know that those mountains, their infinitely mirrored selves, that lake, are still there, exactly the same as they ever were. Nonno's films take us on a tour of the immutable and we are all, without exception, bored stiff. What we want is metamorphosis; we want history; we want the disappeared to reappear and to call us by name and live.

Then, suddenly, there he is! Did you spot him? A wee thing, a capering, puckish scrap in a knitted hat, fitting his round head like an acorn cap, skittering towards us through the high grass of spring. He is all tricked out in an embroidered Tyrolean jacket.

'Oh, Dad, what are you wearing?!'

Miniature lederhosen, knee-length socks, mountain boots: a funny little fellow, your dad: fairy guide, lost boy, sprite; the weightsome, middle-aged man, sitting there in the gloom, transmogrified into an accomplice.

But only for a moment. He's lost again and the fractious, repetitive scratching of the reel takes us back to Nonno's Alps, plotted out by him in all their grandeur. Because Nonno was a successful businessman. Because Nonno was a man with a new movie camera. Because Nonno was a man whose real life was carried out on the street, in the piazza, the office and other, unofficial places, never in company with his children, or that dark-eyed girl, his wife.

How could Nonno's films ever have been concerned with anything less than the Grandeur and Immutability of the Mountains?

On the way home, on the *vaporetto*, moving up the Grand Canal, I watch as tourists diligently record, for their own private posterity, the stones of this ancient city. They stand at the side of the boat, with a camera held about 10 centimetres from their face, and as the boat passes slowly through the water, they film the solemn or exquisite or fanciful façades of the most known sequence of buildings in the world. This is a leaden kind of déjà vu: no Proustian frisson of memory here; no brief glimpse of something from the corner of the eye that has memory springing up, scenting the air and coursing after the disappearing moment, along the winding back alleys. This déjà vu is just what it says: you have already seen it – hundreds upon hundreds of times. There is no surprise, no teasing distance between you and what you see; there is no space left for imagination or memory or speculation to creep in, curl up and grow. Like Nonno's alpine pastures, these lugubrious photographic trawls down the long line of palaces offer only one more reproduction of the thing so ineluctably reproduced.

Often visitors say about Venice: 'It seems unreal. It's like a stage set!'

Now that I live here I no longer feel this because I have gone backstage.

'Throw it away!' I want to say, tapping the tourists bossily on the shoulder, jogging their camera hand, 'Open your eyes. See the unforgettable. It won't let you down: it won't leave you. Don't worry, your mind will keep the pictures safe.' And then I want to add, intrusively, bitchily: 'Do you honestly think anyone is going to want to watch this interminable, moving postcard ever again?'

But really, I wonder if it is less simple than that. Perhaps when the DVD is slotted into the machine (dusty, rescued from the attic) in thirty years' time, those palaces – the impassive, virginal face of Ca' d'Oro, the muscular abrasiveness of Ca' Pesaro – will recall to one person in that dutiful future audience the warmth of a long-lost lover's hand, soft on the back of a soft neck. A pinhead of memory on which dances the last, ectoplasmic puff of a shining first morning, in a cheap hotel room in Venice, when you woke in your lover's arms and saw the reflection of water, moving silver on the wall.

PART 13: August

Paying

DURING THE LONG, hot summer months of July and August, when we are away from Venice with its dense, mudflat heat and increasingly vengeful mosquitoes, the friend of a friend comes to stay in our flat. She is from Milan, where she works for a charity dedicated to the defence of indigenous peoples around the world. She is coming to Venice for the film festival on the Lido, to attend the launch of a film about the Guarani people of South America – displaced, exploited and abused by the interests of power and commerce and whose particular response to this chain of endless disaster is suicide.

Photographs of these people have none of the colourful, primitive drama of the newspaper images of naked men in rainforest clearings, painted red and shooting arrows at aeroplanes. Pictures of the Guarani show dry-eyed boys slumping at noon in the shadow of the sugar cane; men, in shorts and battered trainers, standing in listless groups around a beat-out truck, next to a vast hangar-like building, the sugar cane stretching away in every direction. Defiance and incomprehension have long ago flattened into exhaustion and knowledge. These photographs are neither pretty nor exotic; they exude only a dull despair.

And now, the woman from the charity in Milan has brought a group of Guarani people to Venice, for the public showing of a film that is to reveal their plight to the world.

This is by no means the first time that the politics of human rights has set to work on the Lido. Some years before, Rupert Everett, striding (one imagines) across the strip of sand between his hotel and the Adriatic Sea, a towel slung around his hips, his grand profile, his louche, confident film star's lope, was challenged by some Italian guardian of the beach and told he must pay for the privilege of swimming there. Everett, who, for all his transatlantic glamour, is an Englishman, must have felt a rush of outrage when denied his right to a free dip and, accordingly, kicked up a fine rumpus. The continental notion that the sea must be paid for came head to head with the insular conviction that the sea, chill and brutal, is a democratic right, an individual necessity and the way out – to everywhere. So it was that Everett – Byronic, enraged – stymied in his attempt to swim his own private Bosporus, found himself facing out the signora with the deck chair concession.

I think of all those unflinching, officious faces I have encountered in Italy – in banks, at post offices, police stations, ticket booths – and I am in no doubt that were it not for the fact that Everett is famous and the deck chair lady was not, Everett would not have had the remotest hope of getting his own way.

Meanwhile, when it comes to their own lands, the Guarani have much, much less leverage than the deck chair signora and infinitely more at stake. I am not in their heads; I do not know who they are, nor where they come from. I cannot presume to understand how it felt to these people to leave their home, to fly in an aeroplane for the first time, far away from South America, to step down from that plane in Northern Italy, to rattle in a bus across a long, straight causeway, to a stone city lying low in salt water. I can only guess how they saw Calle del Vin, or how Calle del Vin saw them: the tall, wall-eyed greengrocer on the corner, stacking up empty vegetable crates; the dapper Sicilian who sells cheese and expensive wines; the haberdasher's granddaughter and her cap-sleeved, gold-sloganed tee-shirts, must all have witnessed the arrival of those five small, dark Guarani, shepherded up the *calle* by the woman from the Milan office. The rustling hectares of sugar cane were real only in the mind's eye of the Guarani; it was the grey stone canyons of an aged city that rose up around them now.

I picture them coming to a standstill outside the great wooden door of number 3460. I imagine the woman from Milan jiggling the key in the unfamiliar lock and the scrape of the door as it opens. They enter the dark hall and begin to climb the stairs. When they reach the first landing, they hesitate.

From this point on, I have some concrete information because my neighbour, the saturnine Signor Zambon, tells me, a while afterwards, what happened next.

'I found this group of – of – *Mexicans* – ' he hesitates, puzzled, '– and I said: "who are you?" And they said they were staying in your house. Well, I wasn't sure – but they did seem to know you.'

Whereas Rupert Everett was at least temporarily blocked by the signora with the deck chair concession, the Guarani and their chaperone did succeed in running the gauntlet of Zambon. I see Zambon, with his narrow frame and hunched shoulders; his white, lined, troubled face and suspicious eyes, emerging from his apartment with its ponderous wooden furniture and acres of small lace and bric-a-brac. Arturo Zambon – Venetian hotelier and misanthrope. And I see the short, muscular Guarani, with their straight black hair and wary eyes, and I wonder how any of these people could begin to recognize the human being in the other.

But, in one respect, I may be wrong. Perhaps Zambon, whose budget hotel is cleaned by Filipinas, who have not seen their children since the year before last, is someone the Guarani know very well. Perhaps the Guarani – small, dark, useful, cheap, dispensable – are equally familiar to Zambon.

The world is run by Zambons; the world is fuelled by Guarani. Is there thanks, after all, to be given for the stolid signora, with a deck chair concession, who dared to challenge the Hollywood star and suggest that he, too, should pay for the sea?

Together

EVERY TIME I run into another friend in the street and invite them to my party, I put away the nagging thought that this number of people, and growing, cannot possibly fit into our flat. I try to book a venue – but it's too late – everywhere is taken. So, in the end, there is nothing for it but to borrow a couple of trestle tables from my neighbour, cover them with bright cloths, and have the party in the street.

People start arriving while it is still light. They approach from two directions, at either end of the long *rio terà*, calling out greetings as they draw near with ineffable, Venetian theatricality.

Across the street from our building there is a secondary school housed in an ex-convent. The high, red brick wall is patterned with centuries' worth of opened and closed windows, now all blind, and the bricked-in half smiles of interrupted arches and truncated doorways. As my friends gather, darkness comes. The *rio terà* is like an open-ended room; its ceiling is the hot night sky, spun with stars, smeared over with the Milky Way. Eighty or more people have filled this city room and the warm buzz of their voices carries upwards to the canopy sky, across the canals and the *fondamentas* and the rooftops and out into the black, unlit reaches of the Lagoon, where the grass *barene*, or mudflats, emerge from the water and then fall back again, under the rising tides.

Intoxicated with the pleasure of friends and the heat and food and wine, I have forgotten our bilious neighbour, but at eleven o'clock he sticks his head out of the fourth floor window opposite, like a bearded bad fairy who has not been invited to the party, and starts to bellow furiously down at us:

'Go back to your own houses! You've been making that racket for hours! I'll call the *carabinieri* if you don't clear off back to where you come from!'

The zenophobic undertones are unmistakable, but although he knows that we, the annoying neighbours, are not Venetians, he has not bargained for our Venetian guests.

'You grumpy old bastard!' Federico hurls at him, grinning with pleasure at this unexpected sport, 'this is our city too!'

'Yes,' Marco wades in gleefully. 'Get stuffed, you fool!'

The black-bearded Fairy Malvolio comes back hard and for several minutes the row ricochets back and forth off the ancient stones. But there is not, after all, that much to say once a certain amount of abuse has been hurled by both sides and it is, in fact, the children who have the last word.

Nobody knows how it starts – as far as anyone ever understands not a word is exchanged between them – but as Malvolio's abuse continues to come thick and fast, they begin gathering up the chairs we have brought out into the street. There are about twenty of them, ranging from three-year-old Nicola and Ariele, to Tito who is five, and Costantino and Francesco, to ten-year-old Nico manful on his zimmer frame, and Freddie and Carlo and Gio, Sofia and Esther, Lily and Roland and the big boys, Luca and Michael and Eric.

Silently, they arrange the chairs in a row in the middle of the *rio terà*, directly below Malvolio's window. Then, silently, they all sit down, put their hands on their knees and tip their heads upwards, staring straight at the ranting neighbour. He stops short and returns their stare, astonished.

'And you … and you …' he attempts to start up again, but that solemn, implacable joint gaze seems to have struck him dumb and he merely looks back at them for some minutes more. In the end, he draws his head inside and our children sit on, silently united in outstaring him and his ridiculous rage.

This is a small battle won: the living Venice has pitted itself against the dying Venice. The Venice of the future, determinedly outstaring the past.

If You Care

ALVISE IS IN his mid-sixties. He has the head of Father Christmas: a round, genial face, pink cheeks, kindly eyes, a bald pate and a bushy white beard. But he has the forearms of a rower – strong, muscular

– and a wide-handed grip on the oar.

One afternoon, we are rowing across the Giudecca Canal in a sandolo, one of the traditional boats of the Lagoon, flat-bottomed and unadorned, a sort of small, frumpy gondola. The oars are balanced in the focole, the elegant, wooden rowlocks that look like highly polished stands of driftwood or pieces of abstract sculpture. I am rowing at the front, *prua*, and this makes of me mere muscle power; Alvise, on the other hand, is rowing *poppa*, or steersman, so he stands at the raised back of the boat, expertly twisting the long, heavy oar in the water and keeping us on a straight course.

This is a challenge: the Giudecca Canal is a notoriously choppy waterway; never still because of the constant traffic of large boats – car ferries to the Lido, vaporetti, delivery boats, tour boats and the gargantuan cruise ships that bulldoze through the city twice a day. Sometimes, at the end of a calle leading to the canal, one of these passing monsters blocks out the sky, like a genetically reconstructed dinosaur that has escaped from Jurassic Park and is wreaking havoc in the world of human beings.

'Ha,' says Alvise angrily as we try to stabilize our little craft in the wash of one of these juggernauts. 'They might get around to doing something about those things when one ploughs into Piazza San Marco. Until that happens, there's just too much money to be made. The ecosystem of the Lagoon, the foundations of the city, can go to hell if there's money to be had.'

I am doing all I can to stay upright when the wash from a speeding taxi hits the side of the sandolo and I plump ingloriously down on my bottom.

Eventually, we get across and enter a canal that cuts through the island of the Giudecca. Our oars slice the still water with a lovely ease and we slip out the other side of the island, into the South Lagoon. Ahead, stretching into the distance, are little islands, some abandoned, some inhabited. Cormorants stand on the big wooden posts or bricole that mark the channels of the Lagoon. The lone birds raise their black wings and sit motionless, like small vampires, poised, cape aloft, at the foot of a bed. Sometimes, a small, busy coot pops up through the glassy surface of the water, as though diving upwards from an underwater world.

As the oars move gently and rhythmically in and out of the water, I notice an irritating, distant buzzing sound. The noise increases until we see a motorboat bearing down on us, skimming along the aquatic highway between the bricole. There is a young man at the wheel. Our sandolo starts pitching heavily and Alvise gestures furiously at the boat to slow down; the young man skids by, grinning and shouting.

'Perh!' Alvise snorts. 'They'll destroy Venice with their motorboats. They're no better than the cruise ships.'

As the sandolo stabilizes again and the noise dies away, Alvise says to me, 'Put down your oar for a moment and look over there.'

The summer afternoon has a bright, lemony clarity. In the distance, the city is laid out, a miniature archipelago, its towers and domes afloat on the sea. In this pristine light, the strung out peaks of the Dolomites seem preternaturally close. 'Once, you would have often seen the Dolomites like that. Nowadays, the pollution tends to obscure them. You know,' Alvise says, leaning on his oar, looking out across the water, 'the Lagoon has been like this for a thousand years and it could stay like this for another thousand – if we want it to.'

We talk about Venice's chances of survival, not as a mere monument, but as a living city. He takes the oar and stirs it gently in the water so that the boat begins to turn again, very slowly. 'Shall I tell you something?' he says, smiling. 'The numbers of people speaking Venetian dialect is growing now and do you know why? All the immigrants who come from Eastern Europe to work in Marghera and Mestre are learning it, because that's how everyone communicates in those factories. Tell that to the Lega Nord,' he laughs, 'it's the foreigners who are putting new life into our dialect!'

We are now moving along the back of the Giudecca with its invisible gardens, its convents, monasteries, churches and boatyards; the cranes and winches and broken-down boats awaiting repair – the old Venetian mix of industry and melting, melancholic beauty.

'There are so few Venetians left now,' I say, 'I know it sounds silly, but sometimes I feel guilty just being a foreigner here.'

Alvise shakes his head.

'You say that, but who are the Venetians anyway? Those boys speeding in their motorboats? The carabinieri who play Formula One drivers across the Lagoon? The landlords who drive the residents out with their tourist rents? Or close down the corner shop to let their premises at twice the rate to some guy selling glass made in China to the tourists? They're not Venetians, because they don't give a damn about Venice. They'll suck every last drop of blood out of this city. The real Venetians are the people who live here and help put new life into the community and love this place.' He pauses, then looks straight at me. 'You're a Venetian,' he says.

Epilogue

MOVING ABOUT OUR planet in aeroplanes, we get confused into think-ing things like this: 'Nowhere on earth is further than twenty-four hours away', which might be a useful way of seeing the world, if time and distance were really so easily measurable; but what about the date you never lived flying to Australia, or the day you lived through twice, coming back in the other direction? What about the split second in your life when something was said or done or thought that changed you forever?

Daily life in Bangladesh or Tahiti or Botswana or New Guinea is going on at this moment, just as your daily life is, and mine, but we are separated by more than space. I have threaded my way along an Old Delhi street, beating a path among hawkers and merchants, pick-pockets and mendicants and fat, wealthy women dressed in silk, and thought 'this place is medieval', which was, in fact, from where I stood, no metaphor. The silver bullet of an aeroplane that crosses seas and continents conveys us not only through space but also through time. Through a wall of something finer and more elastic than a spider's web and less comprehensible than the narratives of time or space we think we understand. Our uncertain place in space makes all of us into ghosts. Accidents of birth mean that each one of us is a fugitive in history, lucky or unlucky in the lottery of geography and circumstance.

I grew up loving the stories of C.S. Lewis. They are full of move-ment between different places and times; a wardrobe that opens into elsewhere takes you from inside to outside, from summer to winter, from childhood to adulthood and back again. In *The Magician's Nephew* Lewis invented 'the Wood between the Worlds' where you find yourself outside time and between places, in a land without history. The trees soar majestic and artificial like the nave of a gothic cathedral and are rooted in a flawless, mossy carpet scattered with countless, identical pools. There are no signposts and no clues: each pool is a looking-glass portal into another world. You hold your breath, you jump and you might emerge ... anywhere.

It is with thoughts such as these in mind that I travel. Wherever you are on earth, imagination and attention can reveal what was there – literally – all the time. In any ancient city, in any part of the world, you might pass an unremarkable door set into a wall, glance through it and find a hidden universe unfolding, like an Escher drawing, into arcades, cloisters, gardens. Stepping into a church or a temple or a synagogue, we will come across archaic ceremonies, gorgeously enacted for – as often as not – practically no one. These are ritual routes of access to the past that will bring us into contact with other realities which do not exist in time-frames we can easily understand.

One winter evening in Venice, as I walked past a university library, I looked through the windows at students bent over desks, reading in the glowing pools of light cast by their lamps. It occurred to me, in that unremarkable moment, that I was witnessing human habits and values of scholarship going back in an unbroken line to Alexandria, to ancient Athens, to Babylon and Mesopotamia. Then, two academics hurried by. They were deep in conversation, and as they passed I heard one say urgently to the other: 'What you must take into consideration are the hermeneutics of Byzantium.'

Those scholars could have been ghosts from another Venice, unwinding its life alongside the Venice in which I found myself, though they were dressed in grey suits, not black robes. There is nothing mysterious here: type and tradition, curiosity and endeavour have longer historical trajectories than the few decades of an individual life.

For several centuries now, human beings, in different parts of the world and at different times, have become obsessed with narratives of modernization: the great spring cleaning of civilization. In the twentieth century, the dream of a utopian future mutated into a nightmarish totalitarian present. The idea of progress will always limit human development if it is not leavened with a sense of time's peculiarities – its *timebends* – as Arthur Miller called them – its movement backwards and forwards, up and down, in and out, everything, in fact, that makes up its grand, woven tapestry.

When I became part of real daily life in Venice, I learnt to relish the relationship between the antique fabric of the city and the modern lives unfolding in it. I began to imagine a new manifesto that is, predictably enough, as old as the hills. Might the traditions and ancient narratives of humanity offer us silk routes into the future – or pools – or wardrobes – or whichever metaphor you prefer? Human conventions and customs, manners and behaviour, artefacts and artistry and buildings are all portals we can find in our daily life that reveal, if we stop to look and listen hard enough, our once and future world.

Taking the lived-in, day-to-day Venice as a model might it be possible to refigure the way our culture thinks both about the trajectories of individual lives and of society as a whole? If life and society were seen as something more than a mere banal jog forwards through time, towards extinction, would we be more mindful of who we are and what really matters? And might Venice be allowed to free itself from fantasy and become again, if not exactly ordinary, at least real?